The Inner Image

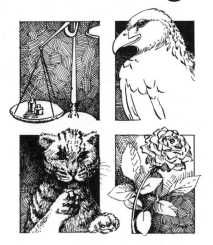

A Resource for Type Development

William Yabroff

Consulting Psychologists Press, Inc.
3803 E. Bayshore Road
Palo Alto, CA 94303

Project Director: Lee Langhammer Law

Content Reviewer: Allen Hammer

Illustration: Daniel Powers

Director Print Production: Laura Ackerman-Shaw

Manufacturing: Gloria Forbes

10 9 8 7 6 5 4 3 2

Library of Congress Cataloging-in-Publication Data

Yabroff, William, 1929–
    The inner image: a resource for type development/ William Yabroff
      p.   cm.
    Includes bibliographical references.
    ISBN 0-89106-045-6 (pbk.)
    1. Typology (Psychology). 2. Imagery (Psychology). 3. Self-realization.
    4. Myers-Briggs Type Indicator. I. Title. [DNLM: 1. Cognition.
    2. Imagination. 3. Personality Assessment. BF 698.9.063 Y111]
BF698.3.Y32   1990
155.2'64--dc20
DNLM/DLC for Library of Congress   90-2665
                                     CIP

Printed in the United States of America

Contents

Preface
vi

Chapter 1
Psychological Type
1

Chapter 2
The Inner Image
33

Chapter 3
Type and the Inner Image
54

Chapter 4
Imagery Insights from the Four Functions
78

Chapter 5
Applications of the Inner Image
104

References
127

Appendix
130

Preface

READERS MAY BE intrigued by a book on psychological type and mental imagery because of an attraction to either field. In the quest for self-understanding and insight, some have used type, while others have used imagery. Both type and imagery draw on the inner resources of people to guide them toward self-understanding and empowerment, and when the two are used together, they are doubly informed and energized.

Today, the widespread use of psychological type extends into such areas as interpersonal communication, conflict resolution, team building, occupational and career planning, teaching and learning, intimate relationships, leadership styles, parenting, and spiritual direction. Similarly, the power of the image is coming to be understood and used in such fields as medicine, sports training, and psychotherapy as well as in such areas as creative problem solving and stress management. It is interesting to note that the inception and rapid growth of professional associations devoted to psychological type and mental imagery have both occurred within the last ten years.

Like many others in my field, I have long used knowledge of psychological type in counseling and teaching, and I prize the insights derived from this approach. Such insights give people an "aha" experience as they discover how much of what they do is a natural expression of their own psychological type. This experience is self-validating and often creates a new context for solving misunderstandings one may have with others.

I became aware, however, that type insights can be all too short-lived—even those derived from the most basic meaning of the four-letter type code obtained through the *Myers-Briggs Type Indicator®* (MBTI®). Old patterns of responding are not easily displaced, and new information, no matter how insightful and helpful at the time, may vanish in the face of interpersonal conflicts or other stressful situations. I began to search for ways to enable the insights gained from type knowledge to be more useful and lasting.

In my own professional training, I was fortunate enough to have received much exposure to the field of mental imagery—in particular, natural spontaneous imagery. I found that inner symbols are powerful communicators that circumvent the conscious mind, thus allowing access to information that is unique and authentic to the person involved.

However, I realized that an imagery encounter often provoked an enthusiastic response—an initial inspiration and "aha" experience—similar to the responses I had observed in connection with psychological type. Those who had worked with imagery might remember that they had had an exciting inner journey, but often would be unable to translate their experience into any sustained practical application.

It occurred to me that since information about psychological type is gathered objectively from behaviors and preferences and imagery is explored subjectively by the inner self, could not these inner and outer worlds be brought together to enable a more effective use of each? This raised a challenging set of research questions. For instance, did the four cognitive functions of sensing, intuition, thinking, and feeling—which form the very foundation of psychological type—have an inner image dimension in the deep roots of the psyche? If so, how might we gain access to this dimension, and what would we find there? How might the inner world be brought into context with the outer, without doing violence to either? How might the insights gained from imagery best be used with psychological type?

With these and other questions, I began a six-year series of research projects at Santa Clara University in Santa Clara,

California, to explore imagery and the four cognitive functions. The research had three phases: The first was to find the appropriate setting and journey for inviting the image of a cognitive function to consciousness; the second explored the insights received; and the third examined the use of the image for type development. In this phase, a deliberate effort was made to consciously apply each function three times per week, rather than letting its effects be left to chance alone.

Participating in these studies were approximately 600 part-time graduate students, ranging in age from 23 to 55 and employed in such fields as teaching, law enforcement, counseling, business, ministry, nursing, personnel training, and computer science. All were busy adults who combined their studies with raising families, working full-time, and meeting the pressures involved in maintaining and advancing their careers.

The research generated a number of interesting findings, which I will summarize as follows:

- The cognitive functions have symbolic dimensions with deep roots in the psyche; they can be accessed to provide a resource of knowledge and experience that would otherwise be unavailable through testing and observation.

- Images of the four functions personalize type knowledge and draw on a host of experiences and perceptions that complement objective type knowledge. This personalized knowledge includes an awareness of one's current use of a particular function and its stage in development. This can lead to suggestions for the next step in growth.

- The use of imagery with the four functions generates attitudinal and behavioral change. Participants reported gaining a new appreciation of their strengths and limitations, which enabled them to maintain a more flexible attitude toward others, establish order in home routines, control resentment toward supervisors in work settings, redirect career plans, initiate new leisure activities, increase the ability to make clear and objective decisions, and negotiate with others of differing types in conflict situations.

- Images continue to be helpful long after the initial imagery experience. Participants reported this to be the case weeks and even months after they had experienced their image, having successfully used it in situations where a particular cognitive function was needed. More systematic follow-up studies need to be done in this area; they will no doubt yield important information for further training and development.

This book is an outgrowth of my research and workshops and presents a method for helping others to find and use their own images. These procedures are continually modified as new data are gathered so that they might be applicable to a wide variety of interested people.

This book comprises five chapters. Chapter 1 discusses the nature of the four cognitive functions as the basic foundation of psychological type. Chapter 2 introduces and defines the nature of the spontaneous image, its roots in the human biosystem, and what we have learned about its use from those who have explored it. Chapter 3 brings cognitive functions and spontaneous images together and shows how the spontaneous image is given a goal and direction for use with psychological type. Chapter 4 illustrates the kinds of insights one can obtain from images of the four cognitive functions. Finally, Chapter 5 discusses the application of the inner image to the practical concerns of daily life and how this strengthens type development.

It is my hope that this book will inspire others to undertake their own exploration of type and imagery and to join in the continuing effort to use both as working partners in the journey.

1

Psychological Type

I would not for anything dispense with this compass [psychological type] on my psychological voyages of discovery.... I value the type theory for the objective reason that it provides a system of comparison and orientation which makes possible something that has long been lacking, a critical psychology.

—Jung, 1971, p. 541

CARL JUNG'S THEORY of psychological type, modified and expanded by Katharine C. Briggs and Isabel Briggs Myers, describes four natural gifts of the mind that influence the ways we perceive and judge life's experiences. I shall briefly summarize type theory in terms of these four gifts, which Jung calls the *cognitive functions*:

Sensing—to know what is
Intuition—to envision what could be
Thinking—to understand what things mean
Feeling—to know what is of value to ourselves and others

Each of these gifts operates in the context of introversion or extraversion. How we use and develop these gifts constitutes psychological type, determines the sequence of type development, and plays a vital role in the success or limitation of our accomplishments.

1

All of us have the potential to develop these gifts. While we use them constantly in daily life, we use some well and others with great difficulty. Perhaps we are unaware of the power and potential of our less developed gifts because cognitive functions do not develop all at once. In childhood, we begin to develop a way of perceiving or judging that becomes pervasive and natural throughout life. In adolescence, adulthood, and maturity, the remaining gifts offer the opportunity to expand what is seen and temper our judgment so that decisions are balanced and wise.

The least developed gift of the mind lies in the hinterland of the unconscious. Its use is difficult at best, often primitive in expression, and may be the source of numerous problems until brought to consciousness and understood.

These gifts of the mind, our inner resources, are great treasures; but like other treasures, they need to be discovered and used. The study of Jung's theory of psychological type is one way to know them and to learn how the knowledge of natural strengths and limitations makes an immense difference in life. Personal development is empowered by a working knowledge of these gifts and by a respectful accommodation of others who use their gifts in a different or opposite manner.

Since the focus of this book is the relationship of imagery to the four cognitive functions, our attention will be on the inner discovery and use of type potential through the development of the most preferred, or *dominant*, function and the adaptation to the least preferred, or *inferior* function. Those who are unfamiliar with Jung's theory of psychological type and the contributions of Isabel Briggs Myers and others may want to refer to the excellent books and articles listed in the Appendix. These resources illuminate how type concepts can be usefully applied to daily living.

Those who do have an understanding of Jung's and Myers' work know that the four functions are the foundation on which type theory and application are built. How they combine and develop, and how the nature of their relationship is defined, distinguish current variations in type theory. However, all who use the four functions in their theories, including Keirsey (Keirsey & Bates, 1984) in his temperament theory, will find the application and use of cognitive functions intensified by the addition of imagery.

The customary approach to discussions of psychological type includes descriptions of the characteristics of each type, the creative use of type differences between people, and the meaning of scores on the *Myers-Briggs Type Indicator*. This approach is appropriate for the constructive expression and understanding of type in the outer world, where classification, accurate identification, and awareness of differences among types are helpful. It is ancillary, however, to the inner symbolic dimension, which seems to manifest itself in wholes and gestalts. The symbols that lie beneath type distinctions illuminate the inner development of the four functions. I shall let external descriptions of type rest with those who have ably dealt with the subject elsewhere.

In this chapter I shall discuss several central themes of psychological type that converge with the use of imagery. After a brief overview, I'll address the nature and process of the four functions, the theory of type development, and the challenge of using the functions consciously in the decisions of daily life.

------■------

Jung's Theory of Psychological Type

Carl Jung, after many years of empirical observation, concluded that two basic "attitudes" describe our response to the environment—those of *introversion* or *extraversion*. The introverted attitude is one of caution, reserve, and reflection. For introverts, meaning comes from within and anchors their sense of reality. In contrast, the extraverted attitude is one of immediate response, adaptability, and involvement. For extraverts, meaning comes from outside and is reinforced by engagement in activities, relationships, and events. The anchor for their sense of reality is external, and their sense of vitality is directly proportional to their participation in the outer world.

These two attitudes direct the orientation of the cognitive functions. That is, a person's introversion or extraversion is reflected in the most fully developed function so that one may be described as an introverted or extraverted thinker, an introverted or extraverted intuitive, and so on, with each of the four functions.

Jung further observed that there are two ways of perceiving experience, both of which he called "irrational." As Jung uses the term, *irrational* does not denote craziness, but rather refers to going *beyond* reason. One way of perceiving is through the five senses and the internal body organs that facilitate awareness of what exists in the moment. This Jung termed *sensation*. The other way of perceiving is through a sixth sense that gives insight into hidden meanings, possibilities, and inferred relationships between people and events. This way of perceiving Jung called *intuition*.

These two ways of perceiving experience are viewed as opposites: Though everyone is capable of perceiving experience in either a sensing or intuitive way, we cannot do both at the same time. It is as if perception were a camera with two lenses, each yielding a different perspective on the world. Although it is possible to switch back and forth between lenses and so view a scene from each perspective, one cannot look through both lenses at once. Then, as individuals develop a predominant use of either sensing or intuition, they take on the characteristics of a sensing or intuitive type in an extraverted or introverted manner. People develop a favorite "lens" according to what seems to be their natural preference and what information they are most comfortable with and seek first; this preferred view seems more "real" than the view seen through the other lens.

Likewise, Jung (1971) concluded that people had two ways of judging experience—*thinking* and *feeling*—both "rational" functions, defined by Jung to mean "that which accords with reason. I conceive reason as an *attitude* whose principle is to conform thought, feeling, and action to objective values" (p. 458, emphasis added). These two functions are the ways people process information and form conclusions.

Jung (1971) noted that "the rational attitude which permits us to declare objective values as valid at all is not the work of the individual subject, but the product of human history" (p. 458). Therefore, both the thinking and feeling functions are objective and relate to universal experience. Jung also viewed them as opposites in that people can use both functions, but not at the same time, and develop a preference for one over the other. The preferred function gives a greater sense of confidence in decisions and is the first approach taken when information must be evaluated. Each of the rational functions is developed in either an extraverted or introverted manner.

In Jung's system, it is important to remember that both ends of the scale—sensing versus intuition and thinking versus feeling—are valued equally. This nonjudgmental quality is an important factor in the usefulness of his classifications. It gives equal validation to persons of differing types and leads them to acknowledge the natural limitations that accompany their own types.

The Contribution of Isabel Briggs Myers

When Katharine C. Briggs and her daughter Isabel Briggs Myers decided to develop a psychological assessment instrument based on Jung's typology—the instrument we now know as the *Myers-Briggs Type Indicator*, or MBTI—they grappled with the problem of how to identify the dominant function. Their ingenious solution was to extend Jung's typology by adding a fourth pair of preferences, Judging (J) and Perceiving (P), making explicit the judgment and perception orientation implicit in Jung's theory. Accordingly, J indicates a preference for planning, order, closure, and resolution of issues through decision making, while P indicates a preference for keeping options open, seeking information, adapting to changes, and spontaneously going along with whatever is happening.

The resulting combination of attitudes and functions produces sixteen identifiable types, the designation for which is a four-letter combination beginning with the basic attitude of attention, E or I (extraversion or introversion), followed by the preferred way of experiencing the world, S or N (sensing or intuition), the preferred way of judging, T or F (thinking or feeling), and the preferred way of interacting with the environment, J or P (judging or perceiving). The two middle letters of the four-letter type designation indicate the preferred functions, describing, for example, whether one is an intuitive–thinking type, an intuitive–feeling type, a sensing–thinking type, or a sensing–feeling type. These are the designations used to describe the types discussed in a later section of this book.

The *Myers-Briggs Type Indicator* brought Jung's typology to a high level of practical application. It was primarily the work of Myers that took Jung's notions of psychological type off the reference shelves of "expert psychologists" and into the hands of people in many fields. Type knowledge is now used to help heal interpersonal conflicts, deepen marriage ties, and lend insight to team building, leadership styles, teaching and learning processes, parenting, career planning, and spiritual direction.

The Meaning and Use of a Function

The term *function* has been elaborated on by Hillman (1971), who noted that it was derived from the Latin *fungi, fungor,* meaning "to perform," with a Sanskrit root (*bhunj*), meaning "enjoy." He combined this with Jung's use of the word and concluded that a function is "a relatively unified, relatively consistent and habitual pattern of performance which enjoys itself in its activity, a pattern that likes to be exercised" (p. 75). Hillman's view underscores an important aspect that is often overlooked—namely, the accompanying natural satisfaction in the exercise of a function.

Such reasoning suggests a natural drive by each function for its own development and a sense of satisfaction when this drive is responded to. This is consistent with findings from my research in the imagery of the four functions, where not infrequently the symbol of a function—even a dominant or well-developed function—sent a strong

Your Preferred Functions

Attitude of attention	*How you like to experience the world*	*How you like to process what you experience*	*How you like to interact with the environment*
E	S	T	J
I	N	F	P

Four-letter type codes based on the MBTI

message to the imager that it needed to be used and trusted more than it had been. The insight obtained from the inner symbol was to let the function become more significant and share a larger part of the individual's life.

However, simply having thoughts, feelings, sensing experiences, or intuitive insights does not necessarily mean that the thinking, feeling, sensing, or intuitive functions are being used. A function is an organizing process that takes thoughts, feelings, and so forth as its content and does something with them. This important aspect of a function relates to its directed and active use.

Jung distinguished between the active and passive use of each of the four cognitive functions. The *active use* entails an act of will and volition, which allows the function to become differentiated and developed. The *passive use* of a function is where one simply reacts to its contents without either conscious deliberation or focused attention. In the passive mode, the function is not used separately but is intermingled with other functions so that one has a jumble of thoughts, feelings, intuition, and sensations without discrimination.

Jung also distinguished between *concrete* and *abstract* perception. I shall discuss this in relation first to the sensing function, then the intuitive function.

According to Jung (1971), "concrete sensation is a reactive phenomenon, while abstract sensation, like every abstraction, is always associated with the *will* (q.v.), i.e., with a sense of direction" (p. 435). Concrete sensing is mixed with thoughts and feelings and is not a pure perception. Abstract sensing detaches itself from thoughts and feelings and discovers what is significant in the perception of an event.

For example, Jung (1971) talked of the observation of a flower. Passively and concretely observed, one would see the flower, its leaves, stem, setting, and so forth, mingled with feelings of attraction or dislike, or perhaps thoughts about what kind of a flower it might be. Abstractly observed, using the sensing function consciously, one "immediately picks out the most salient sensuous attribute of the flower, its brilliant redness, for instance, and makes this the sole or at least the principal content of consciousness, entirely detached from all other admixtures" (p. 462).

This is analogous to conclusions of Newman (1986a), who summarized the nature of perceptual processes as having three levels, namely, (a) perception of the stimulus, (b) comparison of the stimulus with previous experiences, and (c) "a third level, [at which] significance is attached to the stimulus" (p. 4). The third level is reflected in Jung's example above, where the significance of the flower's redness became the focus of attention.

As stated above, Jung (1971) also differentiated between concrete and abstract intuition as either a reactive or a directed process. "Concrete intuition is a reactive process, since it responds directly to the given facts; abstract intuition, like abstract sensation, needs a certain element of direction, an act of the will, or an aim" (p. 453).

Jung also described the judging functions as being either active or passive. Active thinking is will-determined, taking impressions received from sensing or intuition and placing them in a deliberate, logical order. Passive thinking is associative and responds not to a sense of direction but rather takes a direction of its own. It wanders from one representation to another and can even contradict the intention or aim of the thinker; its direction is not logical at all:

I think of my fountain pen, then the aunt who gave me the fountain pen, her green hat, the bird that was as green as her hat, the cage in which the bird lived, the smell of the cage, the next door neighbor, and so on. (Whitmont, 1969, p. 141)

Passive thinking is comparatively unconscious and undirected; it simply happens. It may become fantasy and flower into other creative expressions of the unconscious. Active feeling was defined by Jung (1971) as a

transfer of value from the subject; it is an intentional valuation of the content in accordance with feeling.... Hence active feeling is a *directed* function, an act of the *will* (q.v.), as for instance loving as opposed to being in love. (p. 436)

When one is in love, the feeling possesses the person; the person does not possess the feeling. One is passive, the other active.

Jung's (1971) conclusion was that thinking and feeling "are rational functions insofar as they are decisively influenced by *reflection*" (p. 459, emphasis added). Von Franz and Hillman (1971) added that "a thought may come through the mind, but this is not thinking: one may sit under sad feelings all day but this is not feeling" (p. 76).

Having feelings is one thing, but doing something with them is another. Feelings, here, are the content; how (or if) they are processed—the function—is more important. Many people have thoughts but cannot think them through, or have feelings yet cannot adequately handle them. Von Franz and Hillman (1971) commented that a person who appears to be full of feelings

may not be a "feeling-type" at all, whereas a feeling-type, because he disposes of feelings quite equanimously, may seem utterly devoid of feelings, distant and disinterested. Having feelings and using feeling is the difference between contents and the process which organizes and expresses the contents. (p. 86)

An analogy might be useful here. For instance, take driving a car. A person can sit in the car with the engine idling and only in a loose sense can it be said that this person is driving. It is only after the clutch is engaged that the person is driving the car. To engage the clutch takes a conscious act of will.

Many people experience the functions in idle gear, and this is not wrong. There is a certain enjoyment in being absorbed and immersed in a function. For example, one can become fascinated with the rich colors, textures, and the whole landscape of sensory experiences that surround, say, a flower. Or delight in the symbolic suggestions attending the flower and the landscape.

But it can also be overwhelming. The experience may take on a direction of its own, one that may cause problems. For example, imagine that your teenage daughter or son is quite late coming home one evening and has not called to let you know. This worry creates its own whirlpool of foreboding thoughts as the silence and your child's absence lead you to imagine all kinds of disasters. As the night passes, you find you are almost beside yourself, caught in a widening circle of frightening possibilities. Though spontaneous intuitive hunches may lead to the truth, they may also advance to the point of the bizarre. This passive use of the perceptive function only leads to negative outcomes.

Thus, when individuals have thoughts or feelings, or hear, see, smell, and are simply aware of what is around them, or have an intuition about something, they may be near the area of the mind where the function works, but until they think something through, engage their feelings in a valuation, intensify a sensory experience, or relate an intuition to a meaning pattern, they are in idle, and are not going anywhere with these experiences. Each function has its own natural limitations and boundaries that are magnified if the function is underdeveloped or passively used. As Myers (1980) observed, "The strengths of each type materialize only when the type development is adequate. Otherwise, people are likely to have the characteristic weaknesses of their type, but not much else" (p. 181).

I have emphasized the active and passive use of the functions because it converges with the active and passive use of imagery discussed in the next chapter. If one is to use and develop a function, it takes purposefulness and an act of will. In the next chapter, I shall show how a similar act of volition must be made when using symbolic images of functions to understand and develop them.

----■----

The Four Cognitive Functions

Since the four cognitive functions are fundamental to Jung's theory of psychological type, it is helpful to have some understanding of them to appreciate their gifts and limitations. In my discussion, I shall draw on the work of Van der Hoop (1939) and Newman (1985).

The Gift of Sensing

Sensing and intuition are two ways of perceiving experience. Each recognizes a significant aspect that the other does not. Jung (1971) wrote, "Primarily, therefore, sensation is *sense perception*—perception mediated by the sense organs and 'body-senses' (kinesthetic, vasomotor sensation, etc.)... Because sensation conveys bodily changes to consciousness, it is also representative of physiological impulses" (p. 462).

The sensing function is the original teacher—one's first response to life: to touch, smell, hear, and see, and experience motion, size, nearness, distance, comfort, warmth, cold, pleasure, and pain, all in varying intensities. These constitute data from the five senses and internal messages from body organs, the autonomic nervous system, and those organs responsible for balance and orientation in time and space.

Both Van der Hoop and Newman make explicit an expanded and more active process of sensing in which all input is integrated into a whole, a gestalt of the scene, including inner reactions of emotions and sensations. Such reactions take into account the amount of pain or pleasure, its vividness and intensity, and whether something is out of place, unusual, or threatening.

These experiences are stored in an experiential memory that scans similar past experiences and calls upon the response that was given then before it makes a match for the experience at hand. This enables full attention to be brought to the present without the distraction of thoughts and feelings outside the immediate context.

Thus, the sensing gift is a spontaneous one that includes not only the perception of experience but a response as well, bypassing thought, reflection, the imaginings of intuition, and the values assigned by feeling. When it registers pleasure, the response is self-rewarding, for people may enjoy what they are doing just for the sake of doing it. If it registers pain or threat, the response is to confront, attack, and resolve immediately what is out of place in the gestalt of present reality.

This gift, described as instinctual by Van der Hoop (1939), is a highly sophisticated reaction honed by years of evolutionary survival and adaptation. It is an essential gift of the mind without which life would become dissociated and fragile.

▶   A developed sensing function is most easily acquired by the following types: ISTJ, ESTP, ISFJ, and ESFP. When adequately developed, sensing will manifest itself in the ability to:

- Perceive the whole or gestalt of real situations

- Be present in the here and now

- Delight in pleasures and activities for their own sake

- Note gradations, intensity, color, form, size, distance, and fit

- Drive through to task completion

- Use words and numbers with great accuracy

- Use tools to compute, build, or repair
- Respond immediately with tried and true solutions to problems
- Confront offensive or threatening situations head-on
- Make realistic plans and decisions

Some natural limitations of sensing include:

- An indiscriminate response to all stimuli and events
- View of things in a simplistic right-and-wrong framework
- Becoming locked into single solutions to problems
- Focus on task completion excluding all else
- Difficulty in distinguishing the "forest from the trees"
- Weakness in making plans for the future
- Sense of rush and tension to get as much done as possible

The Gift of Intuition

Like sensing, intuition is a spontaneous perception. It is, however, an insight relating events or ideas to an unseen pattern of meaning. This pattern is experienced as flashes of insight, hunches, the instant rearranging of previous ideas, or a sudden appreciation for interconnections between seemingly unrelated events. It is a response of certainty without reflection and is accompanied by an apprehension that something is true simply because it is true. Jung (1971) observed that intuition

> mediates perceptions in an *unconscious way*.
> Everything, whether outer or inner objects or their relationships, can be the focus of this perception....

In intuition a content presents itself whole and complete, without our being able to explain or discover
how this content came into existence. (p. 453)

Intuitive perception relates primarily to the future and
its possibilities. The intuitive goes backward from the vision
of tomorrow to what seems to be the lesser reality of the
present. Past and current events remain in the background if
they bear directly on the intuitive perception and may be
dropped entirely if not. Von Franz and Hillman (1971) noted
that with intuition, one needs to step back and view things

from afar or vaguely in order to function, so as to
get a certain hunch from the unconscious, to half
shut the eyes and not look at facts too closely. If
one looks at things too precisely, the focus is on facts,
and then the hunch cannot come through. (p. 32)

While sensing experiences reality as physical properties recognized by the five senses and reports on what
prevails in the here and now, intuition finds reality in the
recognition of abstract and symbolic qualities and reports on
what is *not* there but in the realm of possibilities and the
future. As Mamchur (1984) summarized it, "Just as the eye
teaches the mind of the sensing types, the mind teaches the
eye of the intuitive" (p. 4).

These abstract and symbolic perceptions of experience
are stored in what Newman (1986b) called *symbolic memory*,
which allows us to translate them into patterns of meaning.
These patterns are governed by natural structures in the
unconscious called *archetypes*, which give intuitive perception its distinctly human direction. Just as instinct directs the
sensing function and is a vital force in the unconscious, so the
archetype, also a vital force in the unconscious, gives direction to intuitive perception. Such direction results in an
"aha" experience and carries with it a certainty of truth as
authentic as the certainty of the physical object in sense
perception.

▶   A developed intuitive function is most easily acquired
by the following types: INFJ, ENFP, INTJ, and ENTP. When

adequately developed, intuition will manifest itself in the ability to:

- Perceive the whole picture in a flash of insight
- Brainstorm new ways to solve a problem
- Foresee a probable turn of events
- Cut through and find the "bottom line" meaning
- Infer the intent behind words and actions
- Reach out with ever-new possibilities
- Grasp the meanings of symbols and abstract patterns
- Derive visions or inspiration from present fragments

Some natural limitations of intuition include:

- Lack of realism in coping with present problems
- Difficulty in completing tasks before beginning new ones
- Indecision resulting from a vision of too many alternatives
- Lack of commitment due to fear of being "boxed in"
- Lack of awareness of important body messages on care and health
- Tendency to ignore crucial facts and information

The Gift of Thinking

Jung (1971) wrote that "thinking is the psychological function which, following its own laws, brings the contents of ideation into conceptual connection with one another" (p. 481). Newman (1987a) described this process as one of abstracting, from sensing and intuitive images and from already known ideas, "those elements, and relationships, which are consistent with the laws of human logic" (p. 25). Thinking is a way of judging through logic, impersonal analysis, and reason: Principles command loyalty, and logic is the dress for truth. The principles come from reason, which as Jung (1971) noted "is nothing less than man's adaptability to average occurrences, which have gradually been deposited in firmly established complexes of ideas that constitute our objective values.... Everything is 'rational' that accords with these laws, everything that contravenes them is 'irrational' " (p. 459).

Thinking, like intuition, requires distancing or stepping back—as if casting a net into the tide of experience so that we might compare, classify, analyze, define, recognize similarities and differences, measure, understand, and relate to what is already known. Rationality, with its thoughtful reflection, distances the perceiver from the experience so that selected fragments may become the focus of thought within the laws of logic. These laws are easily expressed in words and have a powerful influence over behavior. However, though logical arguments and theories may have an impressive design, they may not encompass reality. As Newman (1987a) pointed out, "Thinking is not so much a way of establishing 'truth' as it is a dynamic process which aims at *more* consistent understanding of the underlying logic of the universe" (p. 25). This dynamic process is governed by cultural norms that prescribe what is reasonable in a conceptual context in a given era.

To thinking types, the sense of time is impersonal, and the past, present, and future have a causal relationship: The past leads to a present that in turn predicts the future. Individual experience is meaningful only when set in this context of historical roots and predictable consequences. In this regard, thinkers develop a particular fondness for continually setting and resetting goals and actively attempt to engage everyone else in this way of structuring experience. Goals and objectives are a natural expression of their particular view that the present is causally linked to what the future might hold—a view not necessarily shared by other types.

▶   A developed thinking function is most easily acquired by the following types: ISTP, ESTJ, INTP, and ENTJ. When adequately developed, the thinking function is expressed in the ability to:

- Understand how parts of a system relate to the whole
- Analyze the flaws or problems in things
- Plan a complete project step by step
- Deliberate through to logical conclusions
- Critically assess the work of others
- Predict the consequences of choices
- Set long-range goals and objectives
- Develop a set of internal principles to organize information
- Explore at the level of theory and abstraction
- Gather information for decision making
- Develop an argument for or against a proposal
- Seek a fair and just solution to a conflict

Some natural limitations of thinking include:

- Difficulty in persuading others of the merits of their ideas
- Tendency to ignore the feelings of others
- Devaluation of ideas or people who do not fit current theory
- Hesitancy to make decisions without endless further study
- Reliance on reason and logic for dealing with all experience
- Inattention to relationship building

The Gift of Feeling

Because the feeling function is often misunderstood—equated with emotion on one hand or intuitive hunches on the other—I shall discuss this function at greater length. Jung (1971) noted that "feeling like thinking is a *rational* function, since values in general are assigned according to the laws of reason, just as concepts in general are formed according to these laws" (p. 435). He wrote shortly thereafter about the difficulty of describing this function. Certainly, of the four functions, feeling is the most difficult to define. Jung (1971) noted that thinking is "incapable of formulating the real nature of feeling in conceptual terms, since thinking belongs to a category incommensurable with feeling; ...We must therefore be content to indicate the limits of the concept" (pp. 435–436).

Unlike thinking with its focus on logic and sequence, feeling is a global and impressionistic cognitive process. The feeling function is important to emotional expression, but is not in itself emotion. It is a complex function, extending beyond the judgment of likes and dislikes. It is sensitive to social interaction, timing, context, tact, taste, and harmonious composition. In thinking, emotional factors are removed or repressed so as to clarify the relationship of ideas and concepts; with feeling, however, emotional factors are expressed and clarify relationships between persons and values.

Feeling is also characterized by a tendency to select aspects of experience that support a harmonious resolution or tone of the situation; it tends to deny or overlook those aspects that do not. This is part of the nature of judging. With thinking, it is often reduced to a matter of right or wrong, logic or illogic. With feeling, it is a matter of inclusion or exclusion, altering and shaping experience so as to fit a value context. As Newman (1987b) wrote, "feeling can either enhance or elaborate upon emotional experiences, or it can repress them out of consciousness" (p. 195).

The aim of feeling is to give depth and value to emotion rather than establish conceptual relations. Von Franz and Hillman (1971) pointed out that "through the feeling function we appreciate a situation, a person, an object, a moment, in terms of value. A prerequisite for feeling is therefore a structure of feeling memory, a set of values, to which the event can be related" (p. 90).

The structure of feeling memory is formed from the flow of the past into the present, involving poignant memories that become like glowing embers in the consciousness of the moment. Names, dates, and places are seldom remembered in sequence. Something that happened years ago may seem as current as the morning. Feeling types process experience through association with similar experiences in the past, through its congruence with personal values set within the gestalt of a current mood or overall feeling. The relevance of any experience to the feeling function is directly proportional to such associations.

Although feeling is closely linked with emotion and experience, it is neither: It takes impressions from these and creates a gestalt whose meaning is greater than that of its parts. This gestalt is somewhat like an attitude that elevates or exalts meaning—for example, sexual attraction becoming love, or anger at an individual turning to indignation about a social issue. It is a matter of judging through personal and universal values. The universal aspects of feeling constitute part of the gestalt, just as universal concepts of logic constitute a part of the thinker's overall structure. As Hillman (1971) explained, feelings "are not 'ours' only. We partake in them, as for instance national feelings and religious feelings. In this sense they are not only something 'in' us, but also something we are 'in,' and which the feeling function can help us sort through" (p. 81).

▶ A developed feeling function is most easily acquired by the following types: ISFP, ESFJ, INFP, and ENFJ. When adequately developed, the feeling function is expressed in the ability to:

- Grasp the whole picture from the tone of a situation
- Appreciate and respond tactfully to a situation
- Negotiate a reconciliation
- Bring enthusiasm and harmony to a group
- Persuade people and sell an idea or project
- Make a decision based on person-centered values
- Communicate an empathic understanding of others
- Explore levels of trust and sharing
- Creatively adapt to the ideals and customs of others
- Give personally relevant meaning to abstract ideas
- Make decisions based on the integrity of personal values

Some natural limitations of feeling include:

- Failure to consider the consequences of choices
- Being caught in personal experience as the sole judge of merit
- Being reluctant to confront others when needed
- Facilitating others' needs at the expense of one's own
- Ignoring data or events that disrupt a sense of harmony
- Being controlled by the mood of the moment
- Misinterpreting objective feedback as personal criticism

---■---

The Theory of Type Development

In the early years of life, each of the four functions has the potential to develop. Sometime during childhood, one of the functions—sensing, intuition, thinking, or feeling—will emerge as the most preferred and become the process naturally used as the primary response pattern. This function becomes the *dominant* function and may develop naturally, if encouraged by accepting parents, or be superseded, distorted, or left undeveloped due to family pressures to conform to some other style.

The Dominant Function

Because the dominant function works most reliably and easily, a child will naturally use it more often. With practice, it emerges as an area of strength and becomes a consistently used resource for activities requiring those strengths. Consequently, the activities lead to a sense of reward, success, and personal satisfaction and come to be favored by that person. In this way, the dominant function is the cornerstone of personality, shaping the interests, values, needs, subjective experience, and outward behavior of the individual.

It is most helpful for people to know which of the four functions is dominant because it embodies our greatest potential strength. Knowing which function is in command provides a consistent frame of reference for life and enables us to use the other gifts in an effective and satisfying way.

A preference is like a muscle or talent in that it needs to be exercised, used, and developed if it is to be helpful to us. Just as a natural talent for something gives us a head start, so a natural preference, say, for thinking, means that we begin with a greater ability to learn and develop thinking skills. The natural preference is not automatically developed, however. If, for example, children have little access to the sort of education that builds thinking skills, they may not develop their thinking ability fully, even when it is their dominant function. Or if children grow up in a family where a natural preference for thinking is not rewarded, they may adapt by developing their feeling side more in an effort to please their parents.

Failure to develop dominant preferences is detrimental to effective life functioning. Though development of the less preferred functions may allow us to perform somewhat adequately, they can never be used as adeptly as the natural preference. Developing natural preferences leads to greater personal satisfaction and makes our best gifts available to others. Myers (1980) addressed this point when she wrote:

> The basic type differences *appear* as differences in interest, but the division goes very deep and rests on a natural tendency to develop in a particular direction and a natural desire for particular goals. Successful development in the natural direction yields not only effectiveness but emotional satisfaction and stability as well, whereas the thwarting of the natural development strikes at both ability and happiness. (p. 189)

The Auxiliary Function

Although a developed and trusted dominant function plays a crucial role in effective life functioning, it alone is not enough. Myers (1980) cautioned that "although the favorite process can be useful by itself, alone it will not be healthy, safe for society, or ultimately satisfying to the individual, because it lacks balance" (p. 182).

By analogy, individuals who use only their dominant function run the risk of living life as a monologue, just as an actor would if he or she insisted on playing all the parts of a drama. Myers (1980) concluded that people must use both perception and judgment:

> Balance does not refer to equality of two processes or of two attitudes; instead, it means superior skill in one, supplemented by a helpful but not competitive skill in the other.... Perception without judgment is

spineless; judgment with no perception is blind. (p. 182)

This second function is known as the *auxiliary* function. The auxiliary function does not compete with the dominant, but rather supplements it, performing its work in support of the dominant.

Good type development involves adequate skill with both a trusted dominant function and a less trusted but reliable auxiliary. One is used for perception; the other is used for judgment. This work involves our ability to make sound decisions. If the dominant function is one of perception, either sensing or intuition, the auxiliary will be a judging function, either thinking or feeling. Without the development of the auxiliary in this case, one will take in a great deal of information but will be unable to analyze and sort it out for decisions that have to be made. Such people will appear "spineless," as Myers indicates in the above quotation, knowing a great deal about the context for a decision but unable to take a stand, to decide, and to order the information by logic or value.

In like manner, if the dominant function is a judging one, either thinking or feeling, the auxiliary will be a perceiving one, either sensing or intuition. If the auxiliary is not developed, one may make decisions, take a stand, and proceed with logical analysis or value priorities, but will lack adequate information to make a sound decision. The decisions made will be "blind," as Myers suggests above, and will suffer from being out of touch with the events where the decision is to impact. Such blind decision makers appear rigid, stubborn, and intractable—quick to decide but quite out of step with what is really going on.

The Least Preferred Function

Jung observed that we use the dominant and auxiliary functions, our strong area of perception and judgment, to make our initial achievement in the world. The other two functions—the *third* or *tertiary*, and the *fourth, least preferred*, or *inferior* function as called by Jung—lie undeveloped, awaiting our attention and use at a later time in life. Of particular concern is the least preferred or inferior function, as it often becomes a source of considerable difficulty. This function is closest to the unconscious, charged with impulsive energy, and quite undifferentiated. If left unattended and unacknowledged, it may express itself in a disruptive, childish manner at the most unexpected times.

Jung (1971) distinguished between differentiated and undifferentiated functions as follows. A *differentiated* function is easily recognized by "its strength, stability, consistency, reliability, and adaptedness" (p. 540). A *less differentiated* function—the least preferred or inferior function of individuals—is known for a

> lack of self-sufficiency and consequent dependence
> on people and circumstances, its disposing us to
> moods and crotchetiness, its unreliable use, its sug-
> gestible and labile character. The inferior function
> always puts us at a disadvantage because we cannot
> direct it, but are rather its victims. (p. 540)

Knowing our least preferred function and that of others is helpful in bringing its potentially destructive power under control. A key characteristic of this function is that its behaviors are often learned by imitation and are not an integral expression of the self. Its skills are difficult to develop, require considerable energy, engender frustration, and may arouse an inordinate sense of failure when used. A full encounter with the least developed function is experienced by some at midlife and is a signal that this function demands serious investigation and use.

To return to the analogy of life as a stage drama and type functions as the players, the dominant function early becomes a major player on center stage, directing all other players—that is, functions—in their parts and giving them more or less importance as a star actor/director might. The auxiliary function is given the chief supporting role. The sensing type, for example, has sensing as the central character and thinking or feeling as the supporting partner; the script, lights, and sets are particularly suited to the talents of this combination. The intuitive, thinking, and feeling types similarly have their own unique productions.

Waiting in the wings, however, will be the dominant type's opposite, the player that our star knows and trusts the least. For the sensing type, this will be intuition; for the intuitive type, it will be sensing, and so forth. Such a player will be given minor roles and used to fill in the general scenario only when necessary.

But suppose this minor background actor has the talent and potential to be a star and wants better parts in the play? Seldom called or consulted, this unappreciated actor may burst forth, commanding attention with new lines and gestures, standing in the spotlight and upstaging the star, who is embarrassed and angry. The star player may tell the audience that it was a mistake, that this upstart actor was not a part of the script and does not fit into the play at all. As the play goes on, the supporting players may rebel, complaining of low pay and uninteresting, insignificant roles. When this happens, they may mount an insurrection, ousting the star from the stage altogether.

So it is with the inferior functions, disrupting unless they are given important tasks to do. But there are natural ways that the least developed function can emerge, most often in the form of awakened interests in the qualities, attitudes, and behaviors associated with that function either in ourselves or others.

For instance, we may become attracted to someone whose strengths are the opposite of our own. Thus, a thinking person might be attracted to a feeling person, an intuitive type to a sensing type, and so forth. In early adulthood, they may start a relationship, as each is strong where the other is weak. In this way, one partner assumes the expression of the least developed function for the other, acting as a sort of teacher or mentor for that time when the partner must express it on his or her own.

Similarly, we may become attracted to the activities associated with the inferior function. So the intuitive type may become fascinated with computers, withdrawing for long periods to explore its uses and mysteries. The feeling person may become absorbed in the study of philosophy and spend hours lost in abstract thought, reading books with titles that would have seemed uninteresting before. The least preferred function has a magnetic quality and may even guide a vocational choice or selection of studies.

Because it is closest to the unconscious, it is also a source of renewal and creativity. Von Franz and Hillman (1971) note that within the inferior function there is a

> great concentration of life, so that as soon as the superior [dominant] function is worn out—begins to rattle and lose oil like an old car—if people succeed in turn to their inferior function, they will rediscover a new potential of life. (p. 11)

The least preferred function may also appear when we feel cornered, frustrated, overtired, or threatened. In this case, it can erupt in highly energized, childlike, or uncontrolled ways that lead others to think "he is not really himself today." In relationships, criticism of a partner's least developed function, no matter how well intended, will lead to a reaction far beyond the ordinary give and take. To the criticized partner, it will feel like an attack on the soul, evoking rage and hurt that can sear a relationship almost beyond repair. Many people who would otherwise work well together unknowingly sever the bonds of trust by attacking their partner's least developed function.

Finally, the least preferred function may appear in the workplace at critical times. Its warning cues are feelings of stress and burnout that occur when a person's natural type strength is offset by job demands that require use of the weakest function. At such times, employees lose energy, feel burned out and stressed, and experience job dissatisfaction and inner devaluation of themselves as people.

Expression of the Least Preferred Function Before describing how the least developed function might express itself, it is important to note that this cannot be easily defined. Certainly it cannot be portrayed as neatly as the skills, gifts, and properties of the other functions. For further discussion, the interested reader is referred to von Franz and Hillman's (1971) excellent article on the inferior function.

▶ **When sensing is dominant**
ESTP, ESFP, ISTJ, ISFJ

The least developed function of sensing types, intuition, will manifest itself through primitive, negative, and even paranoid intuitive hunches. These may be accompanied by frequent physical complaints, frightening visions, imagined disasters, or images of apocalyptic doom. Negative intuition may frequently show up as suspicion and lack of trust in interpersonal relationships; this basic mistrust is not easily quelled by even the most fervent assurances or promises.

▶ **When intuition is dominant**
ENTP, ENFP, INTJ, INFJ

When intuition is dominant, sensing is least developed and will manifest itself in undeveloped and primitive sensory experience. A periodic fascination and absorption with the sensory world may be expressed by binges, addictions, accumulation of wealth and possessions for their own sake, compulsive sexual behavior, or other means of satisfying inner desires. This happens often at the expense of real physical needs. Material security and status may be prized, yet form a constant source of worry. Even when such security exists, it may never seem to be enough, as though there were some unfulfilled symbolic meaning to this striving.

▶ **When thinking is dominant**
ESTJ, ENTJ, ISTP, INTP

When thinking is dominant, the least developed function lies in the inability to express personal values and feelings. Such individuals may adopt "ready-made" feelings that others might see as conventional, banal, and sentimental. Their feelings may disguise themselves as rigid likes or dislikes that others perceive as prejudices; ideas, people, or events that do not fit with the predetermined principles of thinking types may be devalued or ignored. Their interpersonal relationships may remain undeveloped, accompanied by fear of loneliness or rejection and consequent depression due to isolation that may be largely imaginary.

With intimates, the feeling function may express itself as overdependency, possessiveness, or indifference or insensitivity to the needs of those held most dear. Intimacy and passion may be feared, then indulged in to excess in brief escapades.

▶ **When feeling is dominant**
ESFJ, ENFJ, ISFP, INFP

When feeling is dominant, the least developed function is analytic thought that is objective and impersonal. This may give rise to unreasonably dogmatic opinions, vindictiveness, and sudden outbursts that appear rude to others. Such individuals may latch on to a system of thought and "sell" it with loyal devotion as an answer to life's problems, or be overwhelmed by too many ideas and then attempt to oversimplify them by seeking the same theme in everything. Criticism and evaluation by others may frighten feeling types, sometimes to the point of extreme performance anxiety or paralysis; they may in turn defend themselves by self-devaluation.

The purpose of the preceding discussion is to make explicit the outward expression of the inferior function so that we do not ascribe to fate what is within our power to change. One of the surprises of my research in type and imagery was the positive effects people reported when they obtained a personal symbol for their least preferred function: Their natural fear of its disruptive power was resolved and often transformed into a positive attitude of appreciation. This subject will be discussed in Chapter 4.

Summary of Type Development

Good type development involves the emergence of a dominant function accompanied by a complementary auxiliary function. These two comprise an individual's strengths. The gradual development of third and fourth functions occurs through a variety of experiences; if we are conscious of their emergence and do not ignore or repress them, their contribution to our potential can be constructive .

Good type development also involves independent and conscious use of each function in appropriate tasks or situations. It is not an automatic development that we can assume will happen by itself. The conscious and independent use of each function requires not only an awareness of the functions themselves, their gifts, and the activities related to each, but the ability to apply such knowledge to daily life. This is the crux of the matter: How might we apply type theory to maximize each person's potential and best use each gift?

---------■---------

The Challenge of Psychological Type and the Conscious Use of the Functions

At one time or another most of us have wished that we were able to make wiser decisions at critical junctures of our lives. How many times have we said, "I wish I had thought of that," or "Had I known, I wouldn't have done it." In both our personal and business or professional lives, we may all too often have made one-sided decisions because of a lack of information and/or good judgment. Yet we live with our decisions and their consequences sometimes for years.

Life demands that we cope with the here and now, analyze and make decisions, plan for the future, and nurture relationships important to our sense of who we are. Most of us usually attempt to meet these demands unconsciously, out of habit, without calling on our full resources. When a crisis occurs, life requires a more flexible approach—a job or relationship needs the dormant resources of unused functions, a clearer understanding of the situation, and responses that are atypical of our usual style. It is then that we are forced to search beyond our automatic behavior for alternative resources that might rescue an otherwise difficult situation. Too often, however, we come up empty-handed, unsuccessful because the functions that could help us are undeveloped or misused.

If we are to cope effectively with daily life and avoid being called to muster undeveloped resources in crisis situations, then we must begin to use these resources *consciously*. We must also begin to use each function appropriately in the life situation that calls for its special skills, as in the decision model suggested by Isabel Briggs Myers (1980). Here, each function plays its own role in making decisions and solving problems: Sensing gathers the facts, intuition sees alternatives and possibilities, thinking analyzes the consequences of each choice, and feeling weighs the human outcomes of a decision. Myers (1980) believed that the ability to use each function appropriately is a skill that can be acquired:

> The recognition that one process is more appropriate than another in a given situation is an important milestone in type development. Without that recognition, people have no conscious reason to care, or even notice, which process they are using. (p. 201)

In theory, this model of decision making and problem solving has much to offer; however, a considerable gap exists between theory and application. In practice, it may appear that the ability to use each function consciously and purposefully might be granted only to those for whom type knowledge is of primary importance, whose constant attention facilitates recall of which function to use in a given situation. Such persons' knowledge and study of type would thus keep the functions separate and ready for use at the appropriate time.

However, even for those whose interest in and initial exposure to type information have generated a certain amount of enthusiasm, the practical application of a function in an appropriate setting is difficult at best. Most people seldom remember what each function is uniquely suited to do; when decisions must be made, the habit of approaching the situation through the dominant function is so strong that any faint countersignal to switch functions is easily lost.

Simply remembering that it is important to use, say, the feeling or thinking function independently may not be an adequate cue for mobilizing its resources. How are we to bring the correct function into play? By what signal would intuitive types call up the sensing function to gather more information, when their intuition might already be racing toward new ideas or solutions inspired simply by one or two dimly perceived facts? Again, how can thinking types call forth the feeling function, when their analytic minds are eagerly at work on the problem and arriving at a thinking type's solution, aglow with the feeling of rightness about their approach?

The fundamental question is: How can we make functions conscious? And why is it even necessary, since they are natural aspects of the mind in its perceiving and judging capacities? Only when an element is conscious can we use it at our direction and will. If the different functions enable us to deal more effectively with different life tasks and daily demands, our ability to switch from our favored and habitual way of doing things depends entirely on whether we are conscious of other approaches.

Type Knowledge Is Not Enough

Simply *knowing* this, however, is no guarantee that we will be able to use each function appropriately at will. By its very nature, type knowledge is a mental abstraction. We can anchor these abstractions to behaviors and let the behaviors cue us as to what function to use; yet even then, how do we pull that aspect of the mind off the proverbial shelf and use it? Certainly we can pause to remember what we learned about that function, and the more we know, the more we have to draw from. We can tell ourselves, "Switch to the feeling function now," and for some, this seems to shift the inner gears. Nevertheless, this requires that we pause, reflect, and make a deliberate choice. For most who *react* to situations rather than *enact*, this is hard to do.

To complicate the problem, the less preferred functions are not only more difficult to use, requiring patience and effort, but natural attitudes that are framed within the dominant function also come into play, urging disdain for the weaker functions. For example, the sensing type, finding reality in the concrete and here and now, may scorn the intuitive type's sense of the future and its possibilities. Similarly, the intuitive type may come to devalue or find negligible that which is present and apparent. So the planter in the valley may view the visionary on the mountain top as of little worth, while the dreamer on the mountain top may look down upon the workers in the valley and see them as small, limited, and not worth paying much attention to.

In like manner, the dominant framework of thinking may sustain little regard for the feeling function, considering it hardly rational enough to take seriously, while the feeling types may find the thinking type's logic cold, impersonal, and inhumane. So to suggest that one use less developed functions in appropriate situations can exacerbate a basic conflict, which if not addressed will hinder type development and leave the less developed functions resentful of the dominant function's apparently demeaning prejudices.

In essence, plausible as type theory may sound, its practice needs to be carefully considered. The basic question is, How can we put type knowledge into action? Our exploration of the inner dimensions of the four functions is undertaken in light of this question. The strength of the symbol and the image can assist us in this task, for the symbol is a powerful forger of attitudes and a strong motivator of action.

2

The Inner Image

For visualization is the way we think. Before words, images were.
Visualization is the heart of the bio-computer. The human brain
programs and self-programs through its images.

—Samuels & Samuels, 1975, p. xii

THIS CHAPTER WILL explore the language of the inner image, which is a *symbolic system*. Its domain is interior and requires a special approach. I shall describe its base in the human biosystem, discuss its nature and properties, and look at how it has been used as an important resource for self-knowledge in therapeutic settings. This will prepare us to use both the word and symbol with the four cognitive functions of psychological type.

Language and Experience

The purpose of a language system is to conceptualize, communicate, and record experience. A discussion of the various models of human communication would not serve our present purpose. However, an important element common to such models is the notion that experience and its attendant

33

interpretations are processed in three ways: (a) through verbal explanations or descriptions, (b) through a sequence of symbols or pattern of images, and (c) through the body's somatic responses as seen in facial expressions, postures, and gestures.

All of these are language systems: The *verbal system* expresses conscious thought, the *symbolic system* expresses nonverbal thought, and the *somatic system* expresses the responses of the body. As such, the nonverbal system of the image and the body provide a bridge between the unconscious and the conscious world of experience.

When used to express conscious thought processes, verbal systems can organize a vast array of perceptions, behaviors, attitudes, and beliefs, giving context and communicability to individual experiences that would otherwise remain fragmentary. Moreover, we learned in Chapter 1 how Jung, Myers, and others used the verbal system to describe the external world of individual behavior and order it in a theory of psychological type. Indeed, when we stop to consider the myriad individual differences that surround us and how they've been grouped into sixteen psychological types, the ability of verbal systems to abstract and classify experience seems astonishing. Type theory is a superb illustration of how such systems allow rationality to emerge from the limitless flow of psychic and sensory input that would otherwise overwhelm us. It places individual experience as a stable pattern in the fabric common to the culture as a whole.

Like the verbal system, the symbolic system brings order and meaning out of chaos. Its content, however, is not with the external environment; it orders our fragmented inner psychic perceptions. Gordon is quoted by Forisha (1979) in describing how the image brings structure

> out of the terrifying chaos that is the world of sight, sound, smell, taste, touch, and movement. Through the image we sift, select, and render down to a manageable scale both the world of objects and our own human experience. (p. 3)

The Image Precedes the Word

Within the symbolic system, the image, along with the body's somatic response, is the immediate, primary expression of an event. Any experience is immediately encoded in (a) a somatic response and (b) an accompanying image. The verbal system then gives it cognitive meaning and value. The image *captures* the experience; words *report* the experience. The image is a scaffolding upon which thoughts and behaviors are built. In this sense, it is a form of direct perception and experience, and as such, it provides a valuable and direct source of personal knowledge.

Now the idea that an image may communicate knowledge as valuable as the written or spoken word may seem somewhat implausible. When one speaks of the imagination, particularly the visual imagination or the image, it is easy to assume that this refers to something ethereal, unreal, or even childlike. Yet the image system is a common experience in daily life. For example, seeing in our mind's eye the face of a friend on the other end of the telephone line, mentally hearing a melody, visualizing how a coat in a store window might look on us, or night gliding through the dream world, remembering only fragments and mysterious images of people or places the next morning are everyday occurrences. We may also slip into reverie and daydreams to escape the boredom of a banal conversation, a repetitive task, or a long wait at the doctor's office. This kind of imagery does not seem unreal and ethereal.

Thus, many persons associate imagery with daydreaming, which is a passive form of the symbolic system. *Passive imagery* is experienced when we simply allow visual images, with their accompanying feelings and sensations, to fade in and out of focus on the threshold of the conscious mind. In this passive mode, images are memories of places and friends or an expression of an unfulfilled wish and desire; they may compensate for the predictability and ordinariness of daily life.

It is also a matter of common experience that passive daydreaming may allow the imagination to go unbridled and thus become destructive rather than just an idle pastime. Jung (1971) noted that passive fantasies arise from an unconscious process "that is antithetical to consciousness, but invested with approximately the same amount of energy as the conscious attitude, and therefore capable of breaking through the latter's resistance" (p. 428). Jung found that such fantasies often have morbid and disassociative themes that run counter to our conscious motivations and goals.

Suppression of the Symbol System

Along with the association of imagery with daydreaming is an implicit cultural bias in favor of the verbal system. From early childhood, most of us are warned against becoming too absorbed in our imagination. We are urged to concentrate on the tasks at hand—on doing rather than on imagining or reflecting. The young are admonished to focus on "important" matters, such as following instructions from parents and teachers. Though this may be good and much-needed advice, it may also instill an attitude that the symbolic system is a distraction at best or unproductive and trivial at worst.

Thus, learned inhibitions about paying serious attention to inner images and the symbolic system are strong. It is not surprising that we might ask, What does imagery have to do with the real world?

In a poignant essay on the current neglect of the inner image, Forisha (1979) commented that "for most of this century inner has yielded to outer, and words have been proclaimed the proper measure of human beings, and any subjective testimony to the validity of imagery has been swept aside" (p. 2). Further, Don Gerrand, in his introduction to *Seeing with the Mind's Eye* (Samuels & Samuels, 1975), wrote that "the rise of civilization in the last 2,000 years reads like a history of the social suppression of visualization and therefore a denial of one of our most basic mental processes" (p. xi).

Even in the field of psychology, the image is given little value. Watkins (1986) reviewed today's major psychological theories and found that very few indeed value the symbolic system as an authentic source of truth. She pointed to the need for a reconceptualization in psychology to offset the one-sided viewpoint that verbal insights alone lead to health and well-being.

However, none of this is to advocate a return to day-dreaming. Although daydreams may be the form of imagery generally common to most, these authors and others are referring instead to the suppression of the powerful imaging function that takes place below the threshold of fantasy. It is beneath the daydream strata of the symbolic system that the rich and fertile ground of spontaneous imagery is to be found. This imaging power arises when deliberately and actively invited; the responsibility rests on the attitude of the imager.

The discovery that inner images can direct human behavior is not new, but the attempt to deliberately harness this power for constructive purposes is. Once we can become active users of our own imaginations, we can consciously interact with visual images to enrich and inform our experience. This dynamic, active use of imagery has attracted serious attention in both scientific and psychological circles, and recent imagery research is expanding at a rapid pace. Novel applications can be found in the fields of medicine, education, sports training, science, creative problem solving, stress management, and therapy. An excellent summary and review of the research may be found in works by Achterburg (1985) and Sheikh and Jordan (1983). For a broad perspective on the history and use of imagery in healing, psychology, religion, science, the arts, and creativity, the interested reader is referred to the work of Samuels and Samuels (1975).

————■————

The Biological Connection

One factor that makes the conscious and active use of imagery a powerful resource for self-knowledge is its biological or somatic base. Strong links between the image and the human biosystem are a matter of everyday experience. For example, just thinking about biting into a ripe lemon can cause one to salivate.

This link has been confirmed by recent medical research, although the nature of this link remains mysterious. Further, no one is certain exactly what an image is, how it is formed, or where it is "located" in the body. Just what, biologically, is the imagery system? What are its effects on the body and vice versa? Is there an image "generator" in the body somewhere and if so, how does it work? Where and how are images stored? Why do we have images? These are the questions that scientists in fields from physiology to information systems theory are currently attempting to answer.

Parallel Effects on the Body

Early in this century, an American physiologist named Jacobson (1942) demonstrated that a mental image of an activity caused the body to react in much the same way as it does when actually performing the activity. Lying down in a relaxed position, Jacobson's subjects would imagine themselves running while subtle muscle contractions of the muscles used in running were being recorded. Jacobson was one of the first to establish that actual events and mental images of these events share the same nerve pathways from brain to muscles.

Moreover, Jacobson's findings suggested that memory resides in images as well as in the muscles themselves. This idea that mental practice or mental rehearsal through imagery prepares the body for the actual event has today found many uses. Athletes and coaches, for example, use imagery to attune muscle coordination and control, develop concentration, and improve performance. Dick-Read, Lamaze, and others developed natural childbirth methods that rely on imagery rehearsal to identify, control, and release the muscles involved in labor. The well-documented research on the effectiveness of these techniques concurs with the premise that the image-soma link is not just a construct of the imagination.

Effects on the Autonomic System

Since Jacobson, imagery has been shown to affect not only the muscle system, but other anatomical systems as well, including functions governed by the involuntary, or autonomic, nervous system which were previously thought to be outside conscious control. These functions include gastrointestinal and circulatory activity, heartbeat, and pulse rate. For example, one of the most interesting studies of the intimate relationship between the body and mental processes was conducted at the Meninger Clinic, where Dr. E. Green did a series of tests on the yogi Swami Rama. Using sophisticated instrumentation, Green documented the pinpoint control Swami Rama could exert over his autonomic nervous system. Samuels and Samuels (1975, p. 222) cited several examples, perhaps the most dramatic of which was Swami Rama's alteration of heart rate, using conscious mental imaging, from 70 to 300 beats per minute.

In another test, Swami Rama was able to will the temperature on either palm of one hand to vary by 10° F. The warmer side turned bright red, the cooler side turned pale gray. Though an unusual example, it points to the fact that the autonomic nervous system is linked to internal images and supports the use of imagery as an important adjunct to the treatment of chronic pain, peptic ulcers, cancer, heart disease, hypertension, and a host of other stress-related illnesses.

Much of the recent interest in scientific research on imagery has centered on exciting neurological findings, particularly in the area of brain research. For example, Penfield, an English neurosurgeon operating on patients for epilepsy, attached electrodes to the right lobes of their brains (Penfield & Perot, 1963). The patients, who were conscious during the surgery, reported dramatically lifelike experiences of visual and auditory imagery. One patient heard beautiful orchestral music, which she hummed aloud to Penfield. Another heard his mother engaged in a lifelike telephone conversation, while a third relived his visits to friends in South Africa.

Right and Left Brain Theory

Such findings have led to much speculation and have given rise to a number of interesting theories concerning imagery. The most popular concerns the roles of the right and left brain. This theory posits that verbal, linear thought operates from the left hemisphere of the brain while imaginal, nonlinear thought originates from the right hemisphere.

This theory has important implications for the theory of imagery, particularly regarding the question of its location and storage. Sperry (Sperry & Gazzaniag, 1967) was one of the first to study the effects of the commissurotomy or "split-brain" surgery performed on epileptics for the control of violent seizures. Briefly, this operation involved surgically severing the corpus callosum, or the bridge of millions of nerve fibers connecting the left and right cerebral hemispheres. In his studies, which began in the 1950s, Sperry was able to identify exactly which functions were within the domain of each hemisphere. His findings suggest that for most right-handed people, the left hemisphere is the center of analytic thought, that is, logic, verbal ability, and sequential organization, while the right hemisphere is the center of synthetic thought, that is, perception of wholes or gestalts, imagination, pattern recognition, and visual/spatial orientation. Other researchers have used terms such as *active* and *receptive*, or *rational* and *intuitive*, to define left and right brain functions, respectively.

Finally, even those who are convinced that the imagery system is more intimately linked with the right brain agree that both sides of the brain are necessary to process imagery because the left side translates the image to our conscious mind: Imagery could be happening all the time in the right side, but without its translation by the left, we would remain unaware that it went on. Moreover, research suggests that the left hemisphere can selectively inhibit information coming from the right hemisphere by blocking transmission in the corpus callosum.

Imagery, as the right brain's preferred mode of thought, appears to be more deeply linked to the body and to the deeper structures of the brain—most notably, to the limbic system, the processing center of emotions, of the midbrain. This explains one of the central purposes of symbolic language, which is to contribute affective information to abstract verbal thought processes.

Alternative Holographic Theory

Another theory of cognitive functioning integral to imagery theory is Pribram's (1971) holographic theory, which takes into account the seeming anomalies of the imagery/split-brain controversy. He likened the human brain to a hologram, a 3-dimensional image created by a laser beam and in which each part of the picture contains the whole. If a tiny fragment of the image is lost, it can recreate the entire picture because it contains the memory of the whole.

In a similar way, Pribram hypothesized that perhaps images are not stored in neurons in any particular part of the brain, but rather in the *synapses*, in the spaces between neurons; images would thus take the form of waves between the gaps. If so, imaginal information is stored everywhere in the brain. Each image would be like a fragment of a hologram in that it would contain patterns or prototypes of data, just as the word *star-spangled* "stores" the whole song, words, and music. As Achterberg (1985) observed, "When images are regarded in the holographic manner, their omnipotent influence on physical function logically follows. The image, the behavior and the physiological concomitants are a unified aspect of the same phenomenon" (p. 134).

---◼---

Meaning and the Image

No matter how fascinating and persuasive these findings might be, much about imagery remains a mystery. Research into the physiological correlates of the image gives evidence of its biological bases; however, this reveals little about its meaning or impact. No one would argue that when we look at a Van Gogh painting, certain neurons fire along visual pathways in the brain; but to better understand the meaning of imagery, one needs to go far beyond the neuron.

Assagioli (1970), one of the most distinguished researchers in the field of imagery, counseled that one should use the right tools when attempting to reveal the meaning of the image:

> To address the unconscious in logical terms is not particularly effective. In order to reach the unconscious...we have to speak in its own terms. One should attempt to use the mode in which the unconscious normally operates, which is by way of symbols. (p. 180)

He also described the process by which the inner image becomes the vehicle for self-knowledge. The image acts as an accumulator or container of inner experiences, "a complete system of ingathering, storing, transforming, and finally of utilizing energies" (p. 143). This "container" appears to us in the form of a visual image or a symbol, charged with feeling, kinesthetic, and other sense impressions. However, it contains internal life experiences gathered around the pattern of the image. Jung (1971) described it as "a complex structure made up of the most varied material from the most varied sources. It is no conglomerate, however, but a homogeneous product with a meaning of its own" (p. 442).

Another way to explain the power of the image is with the analogy of a magnet. If you scatter iron filings on a sheet of paper, then hold a magnet under the paper, the scattered filings will be pulled into a pattern. The stronger the magnet, the more filings will be pulled toward it. An image acts much like a magnet. A strong image will draw together a large number of inner experiences and perceptions that are stored within. The coming together of these inner experiences constitutes the ingathering power of the symbol.

Active Imagery

Though all images act in this manner, they possess the ingathering and transforming power to varying degrees. For example, the images associated with daydreaming and personal fantasy, which are viewed passively, reside at the surface of consciousness and reflect only the individual's momentary wishes and desires. However, the deeper one goes within and the more active one becomes, the more powerful and useful the images will be. The ingathering power of images at this level is considerably heightened.

Jung (1971) considered the active use of imagery to be among the "highest forms of psychic activity. For here the conscious and unconscious personality of the subject flow together into a common product in which both are united." He added that the process may be "the highest expression of the unity of man's individuality and may even create that individuality by giving perfection to its unity" (p. 428).

The kind of self-knowledge that the image provides under these conditions is deeply personal and cannot be gained through observation, testing, and behaviors in the outer world. Such knowledge includes our individual histories, internal perceptions, our own development, and the aspirations and motivations that are relevant at the time the image is evoked. Such inner images gather threads of experience and weave them into a meaningful whole that becomes like a private language with which to communicate with ourselves. This private language has inner authenticity; it can be truthful without judgment, accurate without seeking approval, and unhesitatingly direct in its message. This active level of imagery is specific, purposeful, and insight-oriented.

This rich resource of personal self-understanding is one of the mysteries that led researchers to explore the imaginal world. Though an image may appear simple or complex to us, highly charged with energy and emotion or as a faintly fleeting figure, its message is surprisingly accurate and detailed once we learn to read its language.

Yet in all this, images embody more than intimate personal wisdom: They have *magnetism*, an ability to attract fragments of experience and recreate and transform them so that they are a living and revitalizing force. Referring to this capacity, Jung described them as *numinous*, that is, infused with a spirit of their own and rendering unique information distinct and different from even a set of clearly explained verbal concepts. Jung (1971) observed that the image "has one great advantage over the clarity of an idea, and that is its vitality. It is a self-activating organism, endowed with generative power" (p. 445).

To entertain the notion that internal images may be alive with their own sense of being and with a presence and direction of their own might be considered by some to be animistic. It certainly surpasses the concept of imagery as a visual picture in the mind's eye. The discovery of life in an image is an experiential finding made by those who fully experience the inner world. Such discoveries reveal that images contain life energy and do not simply mirror external events. Further, they seem to spontaneously arise rather than being created by the conscious mind. When this happens, their meaning goes beyond a single insight or interpretation. The unconscious, therefore, is to be seen not as a storehouse of dead memories but as a rich resource where images thrive and participate in one's life.

Spontaneous Imagery

Until recently, the most serious exploration of active spontaneous imagery has been done outside the United States. Over the past two decades, American psychology has been principally concerned with the influence of the environment on attitudes, beliefs, and behaviors. Measuring such influence has involved the use of experimental designs, intervening variables, and data-gathering techniques. The contributions that came from this research have been of enormous importance, but the symbolic system was not considered a proper subject for study with these methods. However, certain European psychologists, such as Jung and Assagioli, explored the use of spontaneous imagery as a means to facilitate mental health and effect behavioral change. They were concerned about (a) the limitations of using verbal discourse as the only medium for therapy, (b) the long period of treatment needed, and (c) the narrowness of psychological models that excluded higher creative resources usually inaccessible except through symbols and images.

The European researchers had in common three primary assumptions: (a) that spontaneous imagery arises from the situations and conflicts of real life, (b) that the unconscious, when actively and purposefully approached, is a positive resource for self-knowledge and healing, and (c) that the psychic energy contained in the spontaneous image, when brought to conscious awareness, is therapeutic and liberating.

The approach of these pioneers was to have the "imager" enter into a self-generated imagery story as an integral part of therapy, the imagery sequences starting from an initial image or setting, such as a meadow, door, dream symbol, problem, or feeling. The imagery that followed was then allowed to flow freely and was interpreted by a mutual discovery of meaning made by the imager and guide. The imager's own meaning was given primacy. At the end of the exercise, the imager was encouraged to use the insight and wisdom revealed in the image sequences as an authentic and reliable source of inner guidance.

Among the seminal contributions in the understanding and use of spontaneous imagery are Robert Desoille's *directed daydream*, Hanscarl Leuner's *guided affective imagery*, Fretigny and Virel's *oneirodrama*, Carl Jung's *active imagination*, Roberto Assagioli's *guided daydream*, and Martha Crampton's *dialogic technique*. The approach to imagery used in psychological type borrows heavily from these contributions, which I shall briefly explain. The reader is referred to Watkins' (1984) *Waking Dreams* for a full account.

The Directed Daydream: Ascent and Descent Imagery

Desoille (1968), in France, experimented with ascent and descent in imagery, which became the principal therapeutic technique of his *directed daydream*. Ascent here meant an upward movement of images into a mystical light, evoking warm feelings of serenity, joy, and understanding, while descent into caves, dark forests, or oceans evoked nervousness, distress, threatening images, fear, and physical reactions such as rapid breathing, coldness, and accelerated pulse. Descending imagery was viewed as entering the patient's neurotic or problem areas through a symbolic journey unmediated by intellectualization, rationalization, and other self-protective defenses of customary verbal discourse.

Desoille's technique included desensitizing patients to the negative experiences generated through descent imagery until these experiences or images lost their negative emotional charge. Patients were then able to visualize themselves spontaneously "ascending" in positive imagery, which Desoille believed would free them from the difficulties that had brought them into therapy.

Guided Affective Imagery: The Inner Psychic Peacemaker

Leuner's (1969) *guided affective imagery*, developed in Germany, used symbolic scenes that became starting points for spontaneous imagery journeys. The settings were taken from daily life experiences, such as walking in a meadow, used to symbolize a person's current psychic and affective health; climbing a mountain, used to symbolize difficulties and progress in achieving goals; following the course of a river, used to symbolize emotional development and obstacles to self-expression; and discovering a house on a hill, used to symbolize a person's perception of his or her own personality.

Leuner sometimes found it helpful to interact with images. This might be in the form of befriending a threatening image, tiring, exhausting, or killing hostile images, or learning to listen to an inner psychic peacemaker, which usually provided internal guidance and appeared in the form of a wise person, animal, mother figure, or god figure. The patient was asked to allow his or her own benign symbolic figures to act as guides and mentors when appropriate in the treatment process.

The presence of such inner guidance systems, expressed through the messages of wisdom figures, supports the concept that the psyche is by nature directive and purposeful. A parallel finding was reported by an American researcher, Rossman (1984), in using imagery to promote health care. He noted that when inner wisdom figures, which he termed *inner advisors*, were consulted by the patient, helpful information was given that facilitated healing. Rossman (1984) reported a neurological explanation from his friend, Dr. Irving Oyle, author of *The Healing Mind*, who thus explained the inner advisor as a vehicle of communication between the verbal and symbolic system:

> The brain contains approximately 13 billion nerve cells. Maybe two billion are tied up in the speech areas, the parts of ourselves that think rationally, verbally, and call ourselves by our names—the Advisor is the way the other 11 billion cells communicate with those 2 billion. (p. 14)

Oneirodrama: Full Participation

Fretigny and Virel (1968) in France developed a technique called *oneirodrama*. This technique emphasized full participation by the imager in the inner drama and was intensified by experiencing not only visual images, but accompanying sensations and feelings, such as cold, heat, loudness, softness, smells, taste, and body sensations. The Fretignys believed that full identification with the emerging drama was the key to therapeutic progress. Careful attention was paid also to ascent and descent.

Fretigny and Virel also called attention to the varying degrees of direction given by guides during the imagery session, noting that a nondirective stance was most productive for the oneirodrama session. Other helpful interventions ranged from "supported imagery," in which the guide reassured the subject during times of anxiety and suggested means of relieving the stress, to asking questions to help the subject remain in touch with important aspects of the imagery journey—for example, asking subjects to describe an image in detail or to notice something about the image more closely. Finally, there was the use of the fully directed imaginal journey, which included suggesting a specific starting image, asking questions of the image, orienting the image in space, and encouraging images of ascent or descent. Although Fretigny and Virel preferred the nondirected technique, their categorization of degrees of intervention called attention to this important variable in evoking spontaneous imagery.

Active Imagination: Active Participation

Perhaps the most well-known contribution to the use of spontaneous imagery was that of Jung's *active imagination*. Jung (1960) developed this process for patients who had completed therapy, yet wished to continue their personal growth; it was something to be undertaken by oneself, without the participation of trained guides or analysts, though one might use them to discuss the material in a subsequent therapy session. Active imagination was not limited to inner visualization, but included painting, sculpture, writing, dancing, acting, or any other form of self-expression.

In active imagination, the conscious mind is awake and participates by talking with the images, exchanging points of view, asking questions, and even seeking advice from wisdom figures. The images respond with words, movements, and nonverbal messages. The subject can negotiate, take the middle ground between two opposing images' points of view, consciously participate in and follow the flow of the imaginal sequence, and even direct it at times. Images may act as inner mentors, bridging conscious and unconscious meaning systems. As Johnson (1986) described:

> The two levels flow into each other in the field of imagination like two rivers that merge to form one powerful stream. They complement each other; they begin to work together; and, as a result, your totality begins to form itself into a unity. (p. 140)

Jung's contribution to the field of imagery is immense, and to attempt even a summary of his active imagination technique seems almost impudent. However, this fascinating subject has been ably dealt with elsewhere; I will proceed with my discussion of other contributors.

The Guided Daydream: Three Areas of Consciousness

Roberto Assagioli (1970) of Italy, a friend of Jung and founder of psychosynthesis, made full use of the *guided daydream* to promote self-growth. He divided consciousness into three interconnecting levels: higher, middle, and lower. According to Assagioli, *lower consciousness* contained the coordination of body functions, instinctual drives, primitive urges, inferior imaginations, and undeveloped aspects of the self. *Middle consciousness* comprised the conscious thoughts and feelings of everyday life. *Higher consciousness* was where noble and inspired impulses originated, such as artistic and scientific inspiration, elevated intuition, and altruistic love. Because each level has an appropriate group of symbols and images associated with its contents, we can approach it through these respective symbols.

Moreover, Assagioli proposed a number of psychological laws elaborating on how imagery influences behavior and behavior influences imagery. Assagioli's (1970) appreciation of the human imagination led him to conclude that "the imagination, in the precise sense of the function of evoking and creating images, is one of the most important and spontaneously active functions of the human psyche, both in its conscious and unconscious aspects or levels" (p. 144).

The Dialogic Technique: Balancing Insight and Action

Martha Crampton (1978), a student of Assagioli, developed the dialogic method in the use of the guided daydream. A basic tenet of this method is that all images represent some aspect of the person and that one should not destroy, harm, or devalue a negative image but rather find alternative ways to accept and work with it until a positive transformation takes place. The aim is to "work toward reconciliation of antagonistic figures through symbolic identification with the enemy and transforming feared figures by goodwill and empathy" (p. 32). In addition, Crampton emphasized the need to ground imagery both during and after the imagery session. By *grounding*, she means to make conscious the meaning of the image and its concomitant behavioral expression in daily life and, further, to image more mature ways of dealing with the problems involved. She used such techniques as having the imager visualize new behaviors and act "as if" he or she had used such behaviors in real-life situations. She incorporated a wide range of media to express the meaning of the image, such as music, body movement, role rehearsal, and physical actions. "Even within the context of the imagery session itself, it sometimes happens that the subject will move toward a different type of activity, such as spontaneous movement or sounding, which will then be encouraged if it seems appropriate" (p. 34).

Though she was an enthusiastic user of imagery, she was keenly aware of overusing the symbol system at the expense of other forms of therapy and insight. Her monograph is one of the few published guides for training others in the use of spontaneous imagery that includes instructive case transcripts and illustrative materials.

———■———

Attributes of Spontaneous Imagery

We may summarize the attributes of spontaneous imagery as follows:

▶ **It uses all five senses**

Imagery includes visualization, sensing, feeling, hearing, touching, and smell. When fully explored, it can reveal the reality of inner experience that has been lost or distorted. Reclaiming this inner reality has a profound therapeutic effect. Most persons use visualization as their primary access to the imagery world and obtain clear mental pictures; some see faint pictures that can easily be improved with simple practice; a few practice imagery through kinesthetic, auditory, or olfactory modes without an accompanying visual image, which is an equally valid way of imaging.

▶ **Imagery is ongoing and natural**

Imagery is a natural language system, flowing in continuous expression whether we are aware of it or not. It reflects our inner life, yet is seldom far from the "real world." Left unattended, an image may become negative and destructive; given purpose and direction, it may serve as a valuable ally and source of authentic self-knowledge.

▶ **It bypasses the semantic language system**

An image may instantly reveal central meanings or issues without having to unravel the maze of rationalizations, narratives, and distorted perceptions that usually hide such issues.

▶ **Imagery is self-energized**

Images have internal power that contains and generates energy. They have a life of their own in the deep levels of the psyche. When ignored, their unseen influence may become even more powerful than our conscious goals, values, thoughts, and will. When actively invited into conscious interplay, images can become a powerful resource for integration and healing.

▶ **Imagery unifies reality**

There is no distinction between inner and outer reality in the imaginal world. Emotional and somatic responses to images often have the same intensity as the actual event in the physical world.

▶ **Imagery is unrestricted**

The imaginal world is not bound by the ordinary laws of nature. One may breathe underwater, communicate telepathically with images, fly, or change size at will. This facet gives imagery an exceptional facility to deal with core issues without being limited by the physical, external world.

▶ **Imagery is unbounded by time and space**

The imaginal world does not follow linear conceptions of time and space; in this world, time is always present whether the image appears to be of a past or future event. Its presentation is current, bringing both past and future into the living moment. Space is unbounded, and one may instantly ascend to a mountain top or to the farthest star. This fluid use of time and space brings the past and future into new relationships, unlike historical time, which is based on linearity and logical cause and effect.

▶ **Imagery seeks expression**

Images brought to consciousness need to be expressed and applied in the external world; they embody dynamic energy that seeks outward confirmation. Failure to allow such confirmation may cause images to slip back into the unconscious, in time generating a "toxic" response that results in depression or hostility.

▶ **Imagery can glean insights from the personal unconscious**

Descending images penetrate the area of consciousness where insights about the less developed parts of the self, forgotten memories, traumatic experiences, and instinctual drives can be gained. Such insights illuminate current concerns and behaviors that are influenced by early childhood experience.

▶ **Imagery can help us reach the higher unconscious**

Images of ascension reach the area of consciousness where the creative resolution of problems may emerge. Such images evoke higher ethical and spiritual dimensions, give positive support and strength, and allow us to call on inner guidance.

Such a list of attributes enables us to see how such a symbolic system may become an important source of self-knowledge. By making the inner image conscious, we can also access the immediacy of personal and affective experience, often lost in the abstractions basic to verbal systems. We have noted how the symbolic system is rooted in the human biosystem. Though much remains mysterious about this relationship, imagery and the symbolic system are in a more solid reality than ordinarily assumed. Those who wish a further understanding of the image language discussed here are referred to several helpful resources listed in the Appendix. Let us now turn to the relationship between the word and image and consider how this relationship might enrich the use of psychological type.

3

Type and the Inner Image

Experiences in either modality [words or images] may enlighten or imprison us, yet with the interplay of both modalities begins the journey to a full use of human potentialities and the integration of the dichotomies which have fragmented our individual and cultural experience.

—Forisha, 1979, p. 4

THE IMAGE AND the word are interdependent. The difficulty arises when each is used exclusively, words presumed to describe reality and images presumed to describe unreality. In a brilliant essay on the nature of the two language systems, Forisha (1979) stated that when the verbal system alone is used to describe experience, words may indeed enable us to categorize but they also imprison us, giving us only "the form through which we learn to identify rather than see" (p. 2).

The power of the verbal system to bring order out of chaos—its ability to categorize, analyze, and theorize at increasingly abstract levels—is lost when used at the expense of the symbolic system. Abstraction can create too great a distance from the life experience it attempts to express. The use of the verbal system exclusively isolates words from images, severing the link between mind and heart.

The symbolic system allows a return to full life experience, renewing abstract structures by softening their requirement for definition, boundaries, and exclusive categories. The symbolic system does this by contributing a more holistic, synthesizing source of knowledge contained in "the emotional meaning we give to experience, meanings which are often not given verbal structure" (Forisha, 1979, p. 3). Conversely, if we use symbolic language exclusively and fail to relate images to some rational context, the world of symbols may too become a prison, limiting us to the personal and subjective; such use is destructive. Forisha (1979) noted that the imprisoning aspect of imagery arises when it "becomes rigid and intrusive, bringing inappropriate meanings of the past into current experience.... Words separated from imagery cannot be liberating, and imagery without awareness and the interplay of logical process cannot free us from our past" (p. 4).

The two language systems need to function complementarily, each making up for what the other cannot give. Words quickly become abstract recorders of experience, separating us from the personal meaning it once had. Without this personal meaning, words lose their vitality and power. Imagery may express personal meaning, but without a broader context of logical thought and reason this meaning will be lost in the forest of uniquely personal experience. Forisha (1979) concluded:

> Neither words nor images stand solely in the light
> or in the dark. Both explore regions closed to the
> other and open doors through which the other may
> not enter. Either words or images alone become
> polarized and constrictive, limiting our view to a
> partial experience of reality. (p. 4)

In the previous two chapters we explored the fields of psychological type and mental imagery as two sources of self-knowledge, noting how type information is gathered objectively from behaviors and preferences among individuals and groups, and how imagery evolves subjectively from inner experience. Both are vital sources of information—one from testing and observation, the other from inner psychic life.

The foundation of psychological type theory, namely, the four cognitive functions, is crucial in delineating the characteristics of each type according to their functional hierarchy. As type theory increasingly elaborates on patterns of how the functions might relate to each other, the power of such information to be effective could easily diminish in the face of ensuing abstractions.

A partnership between the objective and subjective—between each cognitive function and its inner symbol dimension—offers a solution to this problem. Imagery can bring us back to the inner experience of the functions—the living, personal aspect of the four cognitive gifts of the mind. Thus, each language system empowers the other, strengthening our sources of self-knowledge.

Such a partnership holds much promise as a method of inner exploration. In the pages that follow, I will explain the technique of purposeful imagery as a method for self-discovery based on such a partnership.

———■———

Purposeful Imagery

Purposeful imagery is a form of spontaneous imagery whose procedures I derived from the work of the European image therapists named earlier. Their procedures have been modified for use with psychological type outside the therapeutic setting. The context and direction of the imaginal journeys undertaken by this method are not primarily therapy-oriented in that they do not attempt to explore deep aspects of personal problems except those that might be involved in the use of the four cognitive functions.

In the purposeful imagery procedure I have developed, the use of ascent and descent imagery has been influenced by the work of Desoille, with explorations of Leuner influencing the choice of images used to induce journeys. The inclusion of three areas of consciousness through which the image is deliberately transported is modeled after the work of Assagioli. In specifying the principles of engaging in dialogue with the image and in dealing with resistance, interpretation, and application, I have drawn on the insights of Crampton. The importance of full participation in the imaginal experience is supported by the findings of Fretigny and Virel (1968). Finally, investigation of attitude toward the inner world and one's potential relationship with the image is necessarily based on the work of Jung.

Integrating the contributions of these pioneering researchers, purposeful imagery uses the resources of the conscious mind and will without controlling the image and creates a bridge between the insights of the spontaneous image and outward action so that the inner dimensions of psychological type can be expressed in practical ways. Several aspects of purposeful imagery structure its design and deserve explanation: induction into the imaginal state; dealing with resistance; the importance of a fully participative relationship; principles of interpretation; the three areas of consciousness; and the process of association. Each will be discussed below.

The Induction

The purpose of induction is to take the imager inward to that level of the unconscious appropriate for the issues to be explored. Where the intent is to explore nonpathological, less-defended areas of the unconscious, such as those involved with the four cognitive functions, a medium-intensity induction is appropriate. This should be sufficient to bring the image of each function into awareness and facilitate the interplay of the mind and feelings. This induction need not begin with full body relaxation, as is done when using imagery to augment physical healing, nor should it involve a deep hypnotic state, as is used in the recall of repressed and painful events and where the imager is too passive and dependent to initiate responsible interaction with the image.

A medium-intensity induction is obtained by having the person quietly attend inward, relax, and concentrate on his or her breathing. Noticing and following the breath as one inhales and exhales is an effective way for most to achieve the quiet state essential when working with imagery.

Images reside at various levels of the unconscious, some quite close to conscious awareness and others deeper within the stored layers of inner experience. To what level one journeys in exploring the images of the four functions may determine their power and usefulness later on. For example, if we simply close our eyes and think of an image for intuition, we might see a so-called third eye, a person gazing into a crystal ball, or some other common symbol for intuition. The image might be a combination of several symbols, made up from the fragments of pictures that constantly float on the surface of the mind. Intriguing as these symbols may be, they do not tap deep energies of the unconscious as more truly spontaneous images can.

It is a mistake to assume that depth in imagery can be plumbed by a shallow dive. On the contrary, the inner image needs to be approached and investigated at its own level. If we are to penetrate beneath the surface of the conscious mind, then we must become absorbed in the symbol and be fully present in the inner world, with a willingness to experience whatever this world holds in store.

Most of us have already learned this with verbal language: Think of times when a sentence, paragraph, or even a chapter suddenly came alive and seemed to jump off of the page. At these moments, the reader is receptive and creative—the events of life converge into a fresh context so that new perceptions can spring from previously infertile mental ground. This seldom happens when one merely scans or reads casually or inattentively. Nor does it happen if one's attitude toward the subject is judgmental. The same is true when trying to gain meaning from symbolic language. A casual or critical inner viewing will only yield a series of fleeting images with little meaningful content.

Resistance of the Rational Mind

Experiencing a deeper level of the psyche requires the imager to approach the inner world differently than he or she would approach the outer world. Primarily, one needs to suspend judgment and accept whatever image or experience takes place. It is natural to feel some apprehension about what may be encountered when doing this; such apprehension may keep the imager at the more familiar surface level of the imagination.

Not only do we quite naturally hesitate to venture into the unknown, our rational mind itself seeks to maintain control in subtle ways. For some, the seriousness of the journey itself is a question that lurks almost subliminally in the background of consciousness. Because the mind's most familiar domain is the authority of the rational, outer world, going beyond this domain requires a permission the mind is often reluctant to give.

Another way the mind seeks to maintain control is to itself create an appropriate image for any of the four functions, outwitting the imager by furnishing an image rather than letting one spontaneously emerge. An experiential distinction exists between the two. Made up or created images portray what the imager imagines the function to be and how it is used, while the spontaneous image is a surprise and is less distorted than the one suggested by the mind as appropriate.

The following example of the mind's attempt to control spontaneous imagery was taken from the journal of a sensing–feeling type who wanted to explore her intuitive function. Her mind created a "proper intuitive door" as her starting point. Such a door, she felt, would contain "solid, heavy, natural wood, with weatherbeaten scars [representing] the years of its passage." But when she imagined such a door, she found that she could not open it without great effort; at last it opened, and there was only empty space behind it.

In her frustration, she released her mind's control, and the door changed into a "plain yellow door of tremendous height that disappears in the clouds. I see a small figure standing on tip toes stretching and reaching for the handle. She is afraid she cannot reach it. At this point, the door opens, and there is my intuition, a restless ballet dancer."

The difference between the image of the wooden door and the yellow door represents the difference between a created and spontaneous image. The created image is often intransigent and "frozen" and does not lead to further insight. The spontaneous image flows more easily and leads to a more authentic experience of the function.

Resistance can also be directed toward the guide rather than in relation to the imagery journey itself. The guide may inadvertently bring up unresolved parental issues from childhood or concerns with authority figures. The imager may then struggle with resentment at having to "please" the guide or follow directions. In such cases, guides should make sure to encourage imagers to work for themselves rather than for them. Also, they should refrain from using personal pronouns when leading the imagery journey. For example, "I want you to visualize a meadow" is better rephrased as, "Allow yourself to visualize a meadow." Nondirective attitudes on the part of the guide foster self-reliance and responsibility on the part of participants in the imagery experience and help to deflect the kind of resistance described above.

Full Participation in the Experience

The journey itself should provide the opportunity for full participation in the imagery experience. This opportunity can be initiated by means of a starting image that invites visual, auditory, tactile, and kinesthetic responses, allowing the imager to go beyond simply viewing the starting image. Each imager's access system for his or her own inner symbols can be triggered by one or more of the sensory avenues noted above. Here is an example of how one such starting image, the meadow, can be used:

> Imagine yourself in a meadow. Experience what this is like. Notice what is touching your body, the grass, the air *(tactile)*. Notice any sounds in the meadow, even the sounds of meadow silence *(auditory)*. Notice how you feel in the meadow, letting feelings come

and go *(kinesthetic)*. Now begin to observe, to see around you with more intensity than before *(visual)*. Experience the meadow fully, letting yourself become truly a part of the scene.

Notice how this starting image is used to gain a full sensory response to promote complete participation in the imaginal experience.

Establishing Relationships Within Images charged with fundamental life energy have the potential to influence and direct behavior. Jung (1971) discovered that they are potentialities of great dynamism, and that the preparedness and attitude of the conscious mind determine whether the forces and the images and ideas associated with them tend toward construction or catastrophe.

The "attitude of the conscious mind" refers to our relationship to our inner images. This is more than a matter of technique, though technique is important: It is a matter of how we perceive our images that determines the kind of relationship we will establish. If we believe that they represent unfulfilled wishes and desires, then the relationship will probably be one of critical analysis—we will seek the outward events portrayed in the image. Here, the imager's interpretation is primary and its nature secondary.

If, on the other hand, we perceive the image's nature as primary and its meaning as secondary, the image gains life and meaning of its own beyond the reflection of external events. Then the relationship becomes quite different: One accords the image a certain respect, allows feelings and thoughts to be exchanged, and becomes an equal partner in the mutual exploration of what each has to offer. This is the attitude the European psychologists previously discussed found most significant in the healing power of imagery.

There are two stages in building a relationship to an inner image. The first is to assume the role of an appreciative observer; the second is to establish a vital relationship with the image. This is a natural progression in that once the image is welcomed, sympathetically observed, and the imager becomes absorbed in the experience, a true exchange of psychic energy begins to take place.

▶ Being an appreciative observer

Observing an image carefully and empathically will allow it to fully announce its presence. Images will seldom remain in conscious awareness if observed with an unfriendly or critical eye. Appreciative observation is quite impersonal in its inward stance of acceptance and sincere intent. Such a stance is accompanied by careful observation as one begins to notice important qualities about the image—form, size, color, motion, and context or setting. Without this, little energy or meaning can be exchanged, and there will be a distinct feeling on the part of the imager of being quite separate from the image. The image is likely to fade from memory, and the significance of the entire experience may become questionable.

Appreciative observation precedes, and is distinct from, finding the image's meaning. Vaughan (1979) wrote that an

interpretation is a subtle secondary process which, in the initial stages of working with imagery, is apt to cause problems. Not only does it interfere with the spontaneous flow of imagery, but it can also lead to premature mistaken assumptions which contribute to self-deception rather than intuitive knowledge. (p. 90)

Only after the imagery experience can the insight be placed in the context of conscious thought and behavior.

▶ Establishing a vital relationship

If one has observed the image appreciatively, the second stage—that of establishing a vital relationship with the image—seems to occur naturally. At this stage, a dialogue is established, sometimes with words, sometimes in silence, where questions and answers become intuitive exchanges of both content and affect, including feelings of delight, surprise, bewilderment, distress, and so forth. The image takes on a reality that intensifies the authenticity of the exchange.

· Symbolic identification with the image may also take place. The imager is able to "become" the image, empathizing with its thoughts and feelings. There is a diminishing sense of separation and a growing sense that both imager and image are affected by their interaction. A person may ask for important information from the image, such as its fears, needs, and what gift it might have for one's life, and the image may respond with words, inner hunches, movements, or a meaningful silence. Not only the message, but more importantly, the *presence* of both the image and the imager are mutually exchanged. Later, when the image is revisited, it is easily recalled and often already energized.

The intensity of this vital relationship varies. It may be of such intensity as to form a lasting bond with the imager and light up the unconscious with a numinous outpouring. Most often, the relationship, though beneficial and insightful, fades in and out of consciousness, depending on the extent of its use and on how ready the imager is to attend to the agenda of the inner world.

Principles of Interpretation

Though spontaneous imagery has its own language that we must become aware of, its meaning needs to be translated from the symbolic to the verbal, even though this translation can never be more than partial. The symbolic language is not a code in which each symbol or scene has a singular meaning. Rather, it is the fluid, pictorial representation of living inner experiences clustered around a central theme or subject.

In the interpretation and application process, the image/symbol system is not a substitute for the verbal/rational system, or vice versa. Both are necessary and work best when acting together. Though the image precedes the word and points to meanings beyond the verbal domain, some model or theory of its possible meaning must provide a context for the interplay of both language systems. Jung (1971) commented on this as follows:

Accordingly the image is an expression of the unconscious as well as the conscious situation of the moment. The interpretation of its meaning, therefore, can start neither from the conscious alone nor from the unconscious alone, but only from the reciprocal relationship. (p. 443)

The Importance of a Contextual Model   Interpretation of the spontaneous image in a therapeutic setting is necessarily directed by and conforms to the particular psychological model espoused by the therapist. Such theories provide the verbal context of meaning for the inner image and are essential to the integration of the verbal and symbolic systems. Even the European image therapists, whose work was reviewed in Chapter 2, despite their respect for imagery as a therapeutic tool, interpreted imaginal sequences within their own therapeutic frame of reference.

The interpretation of spontaneous images in nontherapeutic settings, such as when used in connection with psychological type, must be made within a relevant context of meaning. The broad outlines of type theory give sufficient structure for the image to be meaningfully translated, preventing it from becoming a silent guest within the psyche. Nevertheless, every effort must be made to preserve the integrity of the image and the life experience of the imager in the translation process. It is not that one is naming personal, subjective experience as the criterion of truth. The point is that subjective experience is the hallmark of authenticity in the inner world; when it agrees with external knowledge, there is convergence. When it does not, one has two independent sources of knowledge that enrich each other. As Crampton (1969) observed, "Once a person has lived something on the symbolic level, sound interpretation emerging from the person's own experience rather than imposed on him from the outside can add to the value of the experience" (p. 7).

Subjective versus Objective Meaning   Certain approaches suitable for verbal language are inappropriate for symbolic language. For example, if confused about the meaning of a word, we can always consult a dictionary or ask an "expert" for clarification. Yet we cannot ask an expert for the interpretation of an image unless that expert is intimately acquainted with the life experiences and feelings of the imager. A therapist well trained in the use of imagery will always ask for the imager's own insights first, then build on them by showing links and connections with other aspects of the imager's life.

Further, when using words, we have access to synonyms that help explain, define, clarify, enrich, or elaborate on the meaning. Images, however, have no synonyms. We can suggest partial explanations because the two systems overlap somewhat; it is in this common ground that explanations and interpretations can be given. But much of the imagery world cannot be expressed verbally, and meanings must remain within the silent relationship with the living image rather than in discursive analysis. This relationship produces the nonverbal insights and meanings that are clear to the inner psyche yet must remain only partially expressible in words.

> Each time we found ourselves once again on
> familiar ground—thinking we finally know what
> the image is all about—we would have to surrender
> and swim back to it, realizing we had left its depth
> far behind (as we unknowingly had used our own
> means of translation upon it). (Watkins, 1984,
> p. 125)

The image soars beyond verbal definition. Not to allow for this in the interpretation process is to pull a rational net over "the unknown onto its land. There, the subtle is made to seem concrete, the metaphorical literal. This is so not because they are, but because the transposition from their own realm, their own way of knowing, destroys their nature" (Watkins, 1984, p. 124).

This does not mean that the inner world cannot be understood or expressed in words. It *does* mean that there will never be a perfect fit and that the image is always wider, deeper, and more all-encompassing than its well-defined exterior counterpart.

The Role of the Imager The role of the imager in the interpretation process is crucial. In purposeful imagery, interpretation rests primarily on the imager, who is the final authority on interpretation. A guide may assist in the process but should not direct its content. The imager must assume primary responsibility for interpretation because only in this way does the imager make his or her own inner experience "conscious" rather than disowning it or giving the credit for its value and interpretation to another.

The subjective meaning of each function, accessed through its image, is arrived at through the process of free association. This subjective meaning is then linked to whatever the imager knows consciously about the function involved and whatever knowledge about psychological type is accessible to the imager at that time.

Adding Height and Depth to the Four Functions

Another aspect of the image system useful in interpretation is the meaningful interplay of the three areas of consciousness explored by Desoille and developed by Assagioli. In this regard, one might say that, like verbal language, the symbolic language contains a past, present, and future. These temporal categories correspond to the three areas of consciousness and allow imagery to make a special contribution to our working knowledge of the four cognitive functions. In the symbol system, the past and future flow into the present and exert an influence on meaning. To further clarify, let us examine the three areas of consciousness as they are used in the symbolic system.

In exploring the dimensionality of the four cognitive functions, we may gain insight from the realm of *normal awareness,* where we deal with everyday problems; the *personal unconscious* or *lower unconscious,* where instinctual desires, painful childhood experiences, and traumatic events are stored; and the *higher unconscious,* or the *transpersonal realm,* where we may find insights for healing or new perspectives on significant life issues.

For our purposes, we shall examine the three areas of consciousness in terms that dissociate them from their customary use in the therapeutic setting and explore the four functions in a more natural context. These three realms are (a) the realm of daily life, or the present use of a function in workaday concerns; (b) the realm of forgotten memory, or the past perception of that function in childhood and/or its latent power; and (c) the realm of creative resolution, or what the next step might be in the growth and development of that function.

The Realm of Daily Life: What Is Most familiar to us is the realm of daily life, where characteristic behaviors of different psychological types are observed. Here we become aware of type preferences through observing communication styles, decision making styles, and behaviors expressive of priorities and values.

At the symbolic level, images in this area depict not only the current use of the four functions, but whether the functions are overused, underused, in conflict with another, or facilitating or blocking natural type development.

In imagery practice, the realm of daily life may be approached through the starting image of a meadow, beach, house, or door.

The Realm of Forgotten Memory: What Was The realm of forgotten memory and potential includes childhood experiences that were too painful or confusing to remember and thus remain in the domain of forgetfulness until a later time.

Imagery in this area can impart important information about how we were taught to perceive or use a function in early life. It may signal when the development of the dominant function was thwarted, neglected, or underused. It may also signal the potential emergence of unused functions at certain developmental stages.

The area of forgotten memory and potential is often entered in imagery through dimly lit settings, such as a forest, a basement, or underseas. *It is not advisable to explore this level without the help of a trained guide or therapist unless one has had previous experience with imagery.*

The Realm of Creative Resolution: What Could Be   The realm of creative resolution is that of inspiration and aspiration. It may suggest the next step in type development, strengthen confidence in natural type identity, or provide guidance to allow opposite functions to work more harmoniously together. This domain inspires changes in thinking and is infused with strength, love, and freedom. For Jung (1971), it is the area of the *transcendent function*, in which, "when permitted to do so, the psyche transcends reason and the rules of logic, no less than the opposites, for it sees no problem in the simultaneous perception of incompatibilities" (p. 242).

The realm of creative resolution is entered through settings involving focused sunlight or higher elevation, as in ascending a mountain or entering a temple (getting a higher perspective).

Changing realms of consciousness with a starting image in the forest, for example, going then to a meadow, and finally to the mountain, yields a wealth of information about how we use a function in a single image sequence. With this in mind, let us now turn to *association*, the process of interpretation most appropriate for the spontaneous image.

The Process of Association

The image communicates its meaning simultaneously on several levels through its form, message, qualities, function, and purpose. Its *form* is its shape, such as a horse, rock, or restless ballerina; its *message* is a direct, perhaps verbal, communication that is heard or seen within or understood by a silent knowing between image and imager; *qualities* refer to color, lightness, heaviness, and design; *function* relates to the image's motion or action, what it does to attract attention; and *purpose* refers to what the image is for, such as a key, for example, to open something locked, or a closed door to invite entry. These aspects express the image's energy and are the key to its meaning. It is these aspects with which one freely associates meanings and makes from these associated meanings an initial link from the image to experiences of daily life.

Often, we may intuitively know the meaning of our imagery journey after a few moments of reflection. Insights about the form or response of the image, its movement, or a particular outstanding quality may make a bridge to conscious understanding. These first insights will deepen over time as we stay in relationship to the image and begin to use it in daily life.

The following example shows how association gives personal meaning to imagery of a dominant function as we have discussed.

Case Example: *Intuition's Monolith*[*]   Karen's image of her dominant function, intuition, was an eight-foot-high black basalt monolith rising out of a white, misty room. Words had been carved into the stone, but they were illegible; when she questioned it, a mouth appeared on its side and spoke. A pale misty light came in through the windows. The monolith communicated its fear of being ignored and its wish to give her its gifts of strength, certainty, and truth. After the imagery session, she reflected about its meaning as follows:

> This image represents my intuition. I know this because it speaks to me from a mouth and has no other facial features. It is the part of me that knows without seeing and hearing. The mouth and carved words remind me that I must verbalize my intuitive thoughts before I can know what they are saying.

Notice that the function of the image was her first link to its meaning. It spoke to her in a way that reminded her of how she tried to express her intuitive thoughts. She continued:

---

[*] This excerpt and others that follow are reproduced from the journals of research participants with their permission.

Basalt is a dense, hard volcanic rock that issues from the earth's original crust. I see this as being connected to origins, fundamentals, and the creative forces within the earth. I am surprised that my intuition should be made of rock; this implies more strength than I ever thought I had. Seeing my intuition as having such strength and being connected both to the fundamental truth of hard, physical reality and to the ethereal, spiritual truth (the white mist surrounding the monolith) gives me a new sense of wholeness.

Here she began to associate intuition with the qualities of the image that were revealed: dense, hard, volcanic rock springing from the earth's surface. This led to the insight that her intuitive function had great strength and solidity. The fact that the monolith appeared in white mist added a spiritual dimension for her.

Sensing's Embracing Cactus   Karen had a similarly resonant experience after an imagery exploration of her inferior function, sensing. This image also appeared in a room with white mist, but in the center was a large cactus with sharp thorns. When she asked the cactus what it needed, the cactus asked her to embrace it.

I reach up and put my arms around it and close my eyes. It wraps one of its arms around me. The thorns hurt some, but not as much as I had expected! When I open my eyes I see that I am bleeding. We remain in the embrace through the rest of the imagery.

The cactus feared being "cut off" from its base, which was in a large brown wooden tub. She asked several times what gift it had for her but received no reply. Later on in the journey, they are in sunlight—when they've progressed to the realm of creative resolution, and they just stood there, embracing each other.

Karen interpreted her image as follows:

The cactus is a desert plant. When I think of the desert, I think of trackless, unexplored expanses and cactus. So here my cactus is a symbol of the somewhat forbidding, as yet unexplored part of my world. The most striking thing about this cactus is its vitality. It moves, it bends, it is so alive.

It stores water in the desert, and I instantly connect this with water of life. This is an extraordinary cactus, intensely alive and potentially life-giving. It also has the potential to hurt me with its sharp thorns. It towers above me, and its movements are surprising and unpredictable; I would prefer to keep my distance. For it to contact me, I must approach it. This is true in my everyday life as I keep my inferior function at bay by distancing myself from sensing experience!

It's so typical of me while in the grip of my cactus to want a formula or explanation to guide me, something put into words, while ignoring the evidence of my own senses. Its gift to me is my connection with it, that I can approach it, embrace it, let down my defenses and allow myself to be pierced by my sensing experience and not be torn to pieces. My vitality is contained within the unpredictable cactus of my sensing function!

Notice how she again associated her own life experience with the qualities of the cactus, its vitality, and its message to embrace her. This was a personal kind of knowledge about her sensing function, one that might have otherwise been lost had she not sought its inner symbolic dimension.

Questions That Help in Understanding an Image

Not everyone is able to immediately derive meaning from the imagery experience. In these cases, free association in answer to questions linking personal experience to the image might be helpful. Such questions address the image's form, message, quality, and purpose. The following list may be helpful in this discovery process:

- What seems most important to you about the imagery experience?

- What spontaneous associations do you have with the image? Which of them seems most important?

- What is the image *doing* that catches your attention? Does this suggest anything to you about how the function is being used?

- What message is the image trying to communicate about its needs, fears, and gifts? Is there any similarity to your present needs in life?

- What associations do you have with the image in the forest? Do these suggest any early memories about using the function?

- Does the experience in the meadow suggest anything about how you use the function today?

- Does the experience on the mountain or in the sunlight suggest a way you might use the function more effectively?

The imager will find that answers to one or two of the questions may suffice to bridge the gap between symbolic meaning and the conscious mind.

Case Example   To illustrate how freely associating answers to these questions can bring meaning to the imagery experience, consider the transcript below of a 34-year-old teacher and editor who explored the meaning of her feeling function's image, an orange. Notice that she did not have to answer all the questions to understand her image.

First, Julie described her imagery experience:

The Forest (Julie's past): I find a large orange with very thick skin. It lies on the ground. There are dead leaves, ferns, and trees all around. The orange seems out of place.

The Meadow (Julie's present): The orange rolls into the meadow and rises off the ground and hovers near my stomach. Its skin is still very thick.

The Mountain (Julie's future): I bring the orange with me to the mountain top. It is radiant, with very thin skin. I see glowing white seeds near its core. It is so full of life it almost bursts open!

Then, Julie considered these questions as a means of bringing understanding to her image:

Q: *What seems most important to you about the imagery experience?*
A: I can't believe I see an orange. I don't ever think about oranges! Why does it have such thick skin? Why is it hovering above the ground?

Q: *What spontaneous associations do you have with the image?*
A: Nourishing, vitamin C, breakfast, cheerful color, dies in the cold, white blossoms.

Q: *Which of them seems most important?*
A: Nourishing.

Q: *Does this describe how you use feeling today?*
A: I don't know.

Q: *What is the image doing that catches your attention?*
A: It hovers near my stomach and wants me to relate to it.

Q: *Is this similar to something you are doing today?*
A: I feel lonely a lot of the time.

Q: *What does the experience in the meadow suggest about how you use feeling today?*

A: I do have a thick skin. It protects me. I don't express my deeper feelings.

Q: *What does the experience on the mountain suggest about your next step in developing the feeling function?*

A: I need a thinner skin. The orange tells me how my feelings are like seeds to grow new relationships if I express them. When I reach out to others, I feel warm, expansive, and nourished. On the mountain, I feel strong and peaceful. One seed at a time—maybe that is what I can do.

Julie later reported that her childhood was spent caring for her ill mother. She hid her feelings for fear her mother wouldn't love her. "Now I see see why the orange is so thick-skinned and feels out of place in the forest. It describes how I felt as a child." Though her feeling function was naturally introverted in her type, she reasoned that the orange's skin was much thicker than normal and that she was still protecting herself in this manner.

The orange's healing message was more powerful than friendly advice about love and friendships. Julie's inner psyche was giving her guidance. On the mountain, Julie discovered a way to develop this function "one seed at a time." She could then choose to put this insight into action and follow the guidance of her inner wisdom.

Frequently Asked Questions

Several questions are commonly asked about purposeful imagery and should be addressed before examining the imagery of each function in the next chapter. Each question is identified and discussed in its turn.

▶ **Do all types image equally well?**

A common misconception is that intuitive–feeling types have a natural ability to image that other types lack. Though it is true that intuitive–feeling types tend naturally to use the personal unconscious as a source of knowledge, this does not mean that other types cannot travel the same path to great advantage. Jung (1971) observed that imagining and imaging "can come into play in all the basic forms of psychic activity, whether *thinking, feeling, sensation,* or *intuition*" (p. 433).

Sensing and thinking types are typically adept in the use of imagery after they have overcome an initial resistance to taking the inner image seriously. They may have an inherent skepticism that keeps them from even participating in an imagery journey. However, once they have experienced it, most appreciate and value the understanding that follows.

When difficulties arise in obtaining a spontaneous image that is energized, vivid, and stays in the mind's eye during the imagery experience, such difficulties cut across all types—intuitive and feeling types as well as sensing and thinking types.

▶ **Are there correct or proper images for each function?**

In everyday life, certain expressions and symbols typically represent the four functions. For example, intuitive understanding may be represented by a "third eye," and feeling by a heart or a flower. Sensing might be signified by a cluster of grapes representing the wine of Bacchus; thinking may be symbolized by a book or a wise figure with white beard and robe.

In the inner world, there are no correct or incorrect symbols for functions. In fact, almost any symbol may emerge for a function, and often they overlap or appear to be the same for more than one imager. For example, three imagers, each of a different type, could obtain the image of a ballerina for their thinking function. One, a sensing–feeling type, might interpret it to mean precision, control, strength, and grace; another, an intuitive–feeling type, might think of it as a perfectionist drive within; an intuitive–thinking type could interpret it as separateness and independence.

Similarly, a deer might represent strength for a feeling type and tender sentiments for a thinking type. Though the form of an image might be similar, the associated meanings are unique to each imager.

▶ **Does an image represent the whole function or just a part of it?**

No single image can capture the full range of meaning or all the aspects of a cognitive function any more than a single word or phrase might. If we picture a function as a prism in which refracted light creates a rainbow of different colors, each color is a quality or aspect of the light revealed by the prism. The energy within a cognitive function similarly creates a variety of expressions for this function, which are reflected in the imagery.

For example, the intuitive–thinking type discussed earlier visualized a monolith of solid rock for intuition; she perceived and used intuition in that way, and her intuitive insights felt absolutely true and solid, like a monolith. Another intuitive–thinking type might see a cat with darting eyes, looking here, looking there: For him, intuition might mean seeking numerous options. An intuitive–feeling type might see intuition as a restless ballet dancer, struggling to climb an extended ladder high into the air. Intuition in her life might be experienced as an endless search for meaning.

Thus, each image will show one aspect of the function it represents, that aspect being developed and used in the life of the imager. No single image would be adequate to encompass all meanings, and no two persons would give the same meaning to an image for the same function.

▶ **In what way is an image valid for a given function?**

We might ask, How can we be certain that a particular image symbolizes one of the four cognitive functions? Is the image valid and reliable? Validity in imagery is determined by the imager, who alone can decide whether the image is meaningful and truly portrays the inner experience of that function. Thus, validity for the symbolic system is judged subjectively rather than confirmed by general observation and agreement as we do with the verbal system. As to reliability—that is, whether the image will remain the same over time—the answer is probably no. The image of a function will change its shape and form if the imagery journey is repeated even a few days later. Although the form of the image may change, its meaning will remain constant until the individual imager changes by developing that function or changing his or her attitude toward it.

▶ Does knowledge about psychological type influence the image?

Does knowledge about the nature and use of the four functions shape or alter the imagery experience? Purposeful imagery takes place deliberately in an induced state of consciousness so that type knowledge can be bypassed during the imagery experience. If one finds it difficult to achieve such an inward state and gives the conscious mind primary control over the imagery experience, then the image will be influenced by, or even constructed according to, the design that the mind has created.

Will having no knowledge about the four functions detract from the imagery experience? Probably not. Many of the examples cited in the next chapter are reports from persons who were unfamiliar with either Jungian typology or the system of type identification and preferences developed by Katharine C. Briggs and Isabel Briggs Myers. These persons participated in imagery journeys first, then were given type information. No difference appears to exist in either the spontaneity of the image or its authenticity between those who know about psychological type and those who do not.

With these considerations in mind, let us now turn to the imagery of each of the four functions. The examples will show how imagery individualizes a function for the particular developmental stage, needs, and life history of the imager.

4

Imagery Insights
from the Four Functions

The images of the unconscious place a great responsibility upon a man. Failure to understand them, or a shirking of ethical responsibility, deprives him of his wholeness and imposes a painful fragmentariness on his life.

—Jung, 1961, p. 192f.

WE SUGGESTED IN the previous chapter that the symbol and the word might act as partners in our understanding of the mind's four gifts. As the symbol can reveal information not ordinarily accessible to verbal language, use of the symbol clearly enriches our understanding and use of psychological type. In this chapter, I shall report on the variety of insights that have come from the imagery of the four functions elicited during purposeful imagery sessions conducted over the past several years in my research. In addition, I will show how bringing the symbol of a function to consciousness can change a negative attitude toward that function to a positive one. Such change fosters the use of each function's skills and gifts even at a basic level.

Moreover, pairing both verbal and symbolic language to each function provides us the opportunity to reflect, discuss, and find a deeper meaning based on two sources of information, an internal and an external.

In the following examples, the matter of applying imagery insights to daily life situations is left to the imagers, with no specific instructions or discussion. That many did find helpful effects testifies to the power of imagery to influence attitudes and action. In these examples, such effects are random and spontaneous. The deliberate and conscious application of imagery insights is discussed in the next chapter.

The interpretation and meaning of the images are taken directly from participants' reports. At times I shall include my own comments to suggest interesting convergences with type theory. The imager's psychological type is indicated by the dominant and auxiliary function, such as intuitive–feeling or sensing–thinking. Such a designation takes note of the fact that the symbolic system communicates in wholes and gestalts and is seldom concerned with the distinctions of introversion or extraversion, judging or perceiving.

In addition, I shall report on images obtained for other functions that the participants felt were important in their experiences. Remember that images encountered in a forest represent past experience with the function, images encountered in a meadow suggest current uses of the function, and images encountered on a mountain or in sunlight indicate future development. Because past experience with a function is seldom apparent to the imager immediately after the experience, few references to childhood memories will be found in the following examples, even though such experiences did occur with many participants.

Special Note

The limitations of writing about imagery are great and must be acknowledged here. Because the symbolic system is primarily nonverbal, to describe imagery in writing is to describe only the parameters of the image—for example, its characteristics, qualities, colors, form, vividness, and its effects on behavior when used in the outer world. One may also describe those attitudes that we must have toward an image to honor its integrity.

But what is most important about the inner image cannot be communicated in words: its life, presence, and relationship to the family of images within the psyche. This is the essence of the imagery experience, found only by encountering living images during a journey inward.

Another limitation in writing about imagery is that much of an image's meaning is necessarily based on the individual life experience of the imager. We may partially share in that understanding when there is some element common to our own experience. Yet the puzzle remains, for even when similarities of experience exist, each person produces unique images. There is no consensual base of meaning in imagery as there is with words. Our verbal and written language carries with it an implicit agreement about meaning that is supported by dictionary definitions available to all. With images, no such implicit agreement exists.

With this in mind, I trust the reader to know that what follows is the context—the house in which the image dwells. Approaching it with confidence can lead to a rich relationship of renewal and reward.

---------■---------

The Imagery of Sensing Types
ESTP, ESFP, ISTJ, ISFJ

Each function appears to have certain characteristics in imagery. Although these characteristics cannot be used as the single criterion for assigning an image to a given function, some generalizations based on my research can be made.

The characteristics of imagery evoked for the sensing function are marked by very specific images, well-defined boundaries, and a vivid sense of color and form. Examples include metal arms moving in a scissorlike motion, a stately native American, a growling bear, sparkling Greek or Roman baths, an antique writing desk, a book, a harp, an owl, a vibrantly colored peach, a field of flowers, a pile of glowing rocks arranged in distinct designs, a sleek black panther, and a tiger on the prowl.

In the example that follows, the imagery experiences of a sensing type are given for all four functions so that readers can gain an initial view of a complete sequence of images in the functional hierarchy.

Gift from a White Rabbit

Debbie, a 26-year-old sensing–thinking type, was a graduate student in business after having worked in the business world for six years prior. She obtained two images for her sensing function, each representing an important quality of sensing in her life—power, as portrayed by a tiger, and pleasure, as portrayed by a sparkling pool. Her image for thinking, a gentle white stallion, represented her efforts in graduate school to more effectively use that function. Feeling was a repressed function and emerged as an angry beetle that demanded to be released from its outer shell. Her image for the least preferred function, intuition, was a white rabbit. In that encounter, she learned how to use it in a more constructive way.

Sensing: The Tiger and Pool of Water *(Dominant Function)*
Her first image for sensing was a large, strong tiger whom she was able to befriend:

> I got more comfortable around the tiger, who wants my friendship and is afraid of overpowering me. Eventually the tiger lies down and I am able to lean against it to relax. Some kind of alliance develops between us, and from this I can gain the strength and stability of the tiger in my own life.

Her second image was a pool of water in which she swam and played: "The water has energy and responds to me as I [do] to it, as a delicious and sensuous experience. The purpose of our frolic is pure enjoyment and invigoration." She interpreted her images as follows:

The tiger is like me when I sometimes come on too strong with others at work. Afterwards, I feel awkward inside, and wonder why I said what I said. I think I need to make better friends with my tiger. The pool of water is something I do for exercise. I try to swim several times each week, and I enjoy this very much. It is a way I feel good about myself.

Thinking: The White Stallion *(Auxiliary Function)* Debbie's image for the thinking function was a beautiful white stallion

which I have to practice mounting. But once I am on top of it in a secure way, we fly together. I love hugging and feeding it, or just being with it. Once in a while a strong wind blows from the left and its mane unfurls.

When she interpreted her image, she saw in the stallion her own efforts to use the thinking function and her graduate study as one way to nourish that function. She was often unsure of herself and found that once she understood an assignment, she did quite well. The image affirmed her efforts to develop the thinking function.

Feeling: A Giant Angry Beetle *(Tertiary Function)* Her image for feeling was a huge beetlelike creature emerging from a pool of water in the forest:

It has a large mouthful of grinding teeth and stands over me threatening to consume or torture me. In the meadow it reveals that it fears being encased in that awful exterior forever. Underneath exists quite a different being. Hearing this, I begin to cry.

The beetle offers me a pick to crack its outer shell. On the mountain a strong wind blows as I lie next to the creature and I notice parts of its outer shell are blowing away. The color is softening though I cannot see what is beneath.

Debbie interpreted her powerful encounter with a neglected part of herself this way:

My feelings, when they are expressed in their raw form, are overpowering and ugly—which I don't want to acknowledge, much less deal with. In groups that share feelings, I am in a state of panic to keep mine down. If I let go of my protection, will it soften like the beetle?

Debbie was at that stage in life when her third function, feeling, was emerging. It first appeared to her in the forest as an ugly, hard-shelled, beetlelike creature that had been repressed in childhood and now threatened her. When a repressed function begins to emerge, it may do so with considerable force and call attention by its rage. Here, the crust of the beetle slowly cracked and softened until it disappeared and the creature was no longer hostile. It gave her a pick to help liberate it from its imprisoning shell, reminding us that there is a natural drive in each function toward positive and useful expression. She still needed to learn how to integrate the symbolic transformation of the beetle into the real-life expression of her own feelings, but she made a good start through imagery by removing the terror associated with that function.

Intuition: Gift from a White Rabbit *(Least Preferred Function)*   Debbie saw her intuition in the forest as a child-like creature tossed into the air by four trees. It landed on a "catch-cloth and is tossed up again to peer over the treetops at what lie ahead. It fears being tossed too high, missing the catch-cloth, and hitting the ground when it falls back to earth." As the childlike creature began to climb the mountain, it turned into a huge white rabbit on whose back "I can sit as it hops around. I can hold on tight, be warm and safe in its fur, and enjoy the vision from the height of each hop."

When interpreting the image, she reported that her use of intuition was scary and impulsive. She threw caution to the wind, was easily overwhelmed when making intuitive decisions, and later regretted them. Her experience with intuition was anxious and fearful, like the child being thrown high into the air and fearing an inevitable fall to the ground. Through the image of the rabbit, she discovered a way to use her intuition by "maintaining a hold upon reality while experiencing the possibilities, hopes, and dreams for the future. The threat of losing control is greatly diminished."

The least preferred function often results in unusual gifts of insight when addressed at the symbolic level. In this case, the symbolic process was revealed by which she could use and develop her intuition. She could safely gain intuitive insights through the symbol of the warm and secure rabbit. The process as described in the imagery involved taking small leaps, like a rabbit's hop, rather than a frightening flight and plunge as represented by the child hurled into the air. The rabbit was an image that she trusted. That brought about a new attitude toward her intuition and opened the door for its more constructive use.

Expanding One's View

The image of a 33-year-old engineer, Tom, a sensing type, suggested that he might have been overly confined and rigid and that his sensing function needed expanded use to be productive. If overused, a strongly developed sensing function imprisons one in a harsh practicality.

Sensing: The Ropes and the Elephant *(Dominant Function)*
The engineer was taken by surprise in the encounter with
his image for sensing.

> In the forest is a one-room cottage. As I look
> inside, I suddenly realize that the person inside
> is an image of myself. He has a big smile on his
> face and yet he is wrapped very neatly from neck
> to waist with a heavy rope. In the meadow, it
> changes to a large, lumbering elephant. We go up
> a steep mountain path, and I ride the elephant all
> the way to the top, where the elephant wishes me
> to be by myself.

Tom interpreted his encounter this way:

> I find this image significant and accurate. It is my
> war between anxiety and inner peace that I have
> struggled with for a number of years. The solution
> seems so simple—to just loosen the ropes that are
> binding me from being myself. I feel constrained by
> my view of the world. As for the elephant, I have a
> sense that it came to take me up on the mountain.
> Its gifts are maturity, wisdom, and certainty, and
> it needs my cooperation to have a deeper insight
> in my life.

Feeling: The Empty Vase *(Tertiary Function)*   The image
for his feeling function was a large empty vase.

> I am overwhelmed by this huge, oriental-looking
> blue pot. It can hold a tremendous amount, and
> yet is empty! I leave the vase and venture up the
> mountain. Waiting for me at the top is a spiritual
> father. He simply stands there looking at me. With
> him I know of my need for the gift of personal
> intimacy.

The following week, he reported a spontaneous effect in
which he found himself more responsive to his wife's needs

and was now ready to talk about untouched matters that had stood between them for years.

Intuition: The Flying Creature *(Least Preferred Function)*
His image for intuition emerged in an unusual form: a creature with a giraffe's head, large wings, and a brownish body. With the engineer on its back, it began to fly and showed him a vision from the mountaintop. "I become aware of the creature's awesome wings and long legs that enable it to walk. As we start the mountain ascent, I am invited to climb on the creature's back and fly to the top with ease. I am now seeing another dimension of the same image as it is flying."

His image showed him a graphic sensing view of the intuitive process, which he interpreted as follows:

> The creature conveys to me qualities of complexity in having different physical parts, looking like a caterpillar, giraffe, and butterfly, all wrapped into one. Still being one creature, it can function in a number of different ways, like crawling, walking, and flying. On the mountain, where I can see everything, it is very graceful and soaring. The creature gives me that same ability to see things at a distance.

He was surprised at how clearly the flying creature portrayed intuition from his frame of reference. This understanding was a precursor to future constructive uses of intuition. He summarized his imagery experiences as follows:

> I have become keenly aware of numerous untapped resources in relating to people and my means of expression. I am confronted with the need to explore areas in my life and also recognize that resistance to move in this direction is both internal and external. Life has much more to offer in a continual renewing of my body, mind, and spirit.

The Imagery of Intuitive Types
ENTP, ENFP, INTJ, INFJ

Images of intuition are often characterized by motion or energy emanating from within. Examples include a sea gull, a waterfall in the sunlight, a firefly, a stream of clear water flowing among rocks, a large butterfly in flight, an undulating snakelike coil of golden light, a burning candle, a multicolored diamond revolving in the sunlight, a buddha flooded by sunlight, a woman flying with butterfly wings, a soaring blue heron, and a questing knight.

The Questing Knight

The following example concerns Nancy, an intuitive–feeling type who had left her job after ten years as an operations supervisor with the Social Security Administration. She enjoyed being available and close to her employees, but was continually criticized by supervisors for taking their personal concerns too seriously as part of her job. She was seeking another position that would give her an opportunity to be more person-oriented.

Her image for intuition, a knight, was balanced by its sensing opposite, a three-headed dog. This is an interesting illustration of a balancing effect that the least preferred function may have on the dominant so that they work together cooperatively rather than in conflict.

Intuition: The Questing Knight *(Dominant Function)*   Her image for her intuition was a knight in silver armor who told her that he yearned to embark on quests for the "good of his soul and for mankind." He needed brotherhood to "be understood in his deepest self, to talk about things which most people don't care about." He feared not having value in the world and always being alone, isolated, and without purpose. His gift was "courage, determination, devotion to the quest, loyalty, internal peace—all for the purpose of finding meaning. The quest itself is the purpose."

The woman began to use her image of the white knight as she evaluated her job:

> I use him to help me let go of former beliefs and
> not be so self-critical because I don't fit the standard
> ESTJ business-manager format. I'm looking at myself
> with a much greater sense of, "So this is the way I
> am, and that's just as good as all the ESTJ's in the
> world!" My white knight helps me value qualities
> which are strengths, although I have never found
> support before in seeing them as strengths.

Sensing: A Three-Headed Dog *(Least Preferred Function)*
Her image for the sensing function was a fierce three-headed dog racing around in circles; she learned that it needed "expression" but was not sure what that meant. "Cerberus looks in all directions and doesn't miss a thing.... This is very 'sensing' to me. When I operate in this mode, I growl more because it takes so much energy to see what's happening, what's wrong, and how to fix it." The three-headed dog gave her a special gift—"to keep the knight from wandering with his head in the clouds." In the sunlight, the dog changed into a lone wolf "who comes to me and I put my arms around him, for we are now friends."

This woman related strongly to the questing knight's desire to do something of profound significance. This characteristic of intuitive types needs be honored if they are to find satisfaction in life and work. The knight asked her to share her vision with others to find support for her ideals.

Her least preferred function, sensing, whose image was a three-headed dog, illustrated how this function often gives balance to intuition. The dog helped the knight to keep his "feet on the ground and not get lost in the clouds," as she put it. That symbol gave her a new appreciation for checking her visions against reality—a helpful process for an intuitive to learn.

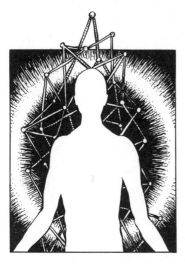

The Pattern of Life

The next example illustrates the first imagery experience of an intuitive–thinking type who was skeptical about the inner world. Ken, a 53-year-old electrical engineer, took pride in being rational, scientific, and down-to-earth. Despite his skepticism about the use of imagery, he decided to participate in the journey with the attitude that he was "exploring unfamiliar territory" rather than undertaking a foolish endeavor.

Intuition: The Growing Puzzle *(Dominant Function)*   In his first experience, he encountered an image of intuition described as a multitude of line segments joining each other in an open ellipse that was connected to him by a membrane. He was awed by the living quality of the figure, which moved close to him and began to radiate light. The membrane disappeared as the figure approached. He interpreted his image with an enthusiasm surprising after his initial skepticism:

> This figure represents my life pattern! I am taking short paths in many directions.·At first, this seems aimless, chaotic. Then I see connections between paths. I regret passing so quickly from one path to another. I call this image My Growing Puzzle. Its ambiguity fits me.

The following week, Ken reported certain spontaneous effects that took place since his encounter with intuition:

> I have new free-flowing ideas. I complete a metal sculpture in a short time, have two conversations that resolve anger and conflict, feel easy with myself, and am more confident in my ability to fit my life pattern together. This feeling may last only a minute more, or it may go on for days, weeks, or months. Who knows?

Of particular interest is Ken's willingness to set aside his skepticism and adopt an open, exploring attitude. Moreover, he was willing to accept whatever image spontaneously emerged. In the beginning, participants often expect some brilliantly colored image to appear and may be disappointed if this does not happen. Any image, whether an exotic picture or a simple outline, may be significant.

We might also note that although the engineer was an intuitive–thinking type he had considerable distrust of intuition. As he accepted the pattern of lines, the distance between the two, represented by the membrane, disappeared, and he was able to find new energies in the function.

———■———

The Images of Thinking Types
ESTJ, ENTJ, ISTP, INTP

The imagery of thinking is similar to that of sensing in that it often has clearly defined boundaries and distinct images; however, it is often more ordered, complex, or focused. Examples of thinking images include an ancient stone, a black pyramid, a diamond, a caterpillar, a brick wall, a butterfly, a stone tablet, a bow and arrow, a drill, a tiger's jaw, a lion, a large fish net, a nautilus shell, and an eyeless sage.

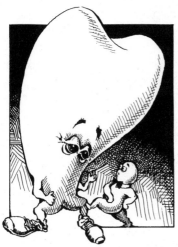

The Resolution of Hostile Images

The following example was taken from Bill, a thinking–sensing type who was a college instructor in the biological sciences as well as a serious horticulturist. He took five imagery journeys, the first with a guide, the last four conducted by himself at his home. His experience illustrates two important points—first, that one can continue imagery work independently with productive results, and second, that a weaker function needs to be symbolically acknowledged and strengthened before it will cooperate with its dominant counterpart.

Sensing: A Large, Stern Blob (*Auxiliary Function*)   Bill encountered his sensing function as a large, stern "blob" with legs, hands, and a head. The large "blob" brusquely called out, "Get busy and don't waste time! Accomplish your goals!"

Intuition: A Small, Angry Blob (*Tertiary Function*)   A small blob, similar to the large one, emerged as an image of the instructor's intuition. As a less developed function, it attempted to get past the large blob which was blocking its view, but to no avail. When the imager asked why it was stuck behind the large blob, it said, "You know why; don't bother to ask!"

In the next four sessions done at home, the small blob continued its hostility toward the large one, kicking it on the shins and hitting it on the head as they chased and yelled at each other. The imager persisted in talking with them for a short time each day. They became more human and began to look like the imager himself. Their stern message to "Get busy!" or to "Get out of my way!" began to change.

In the last session, both blobs asked to join him in the sunlight. They had a long conversation and finally made peace all around. They told the imager that peace required him to be willing to talk with and accept them both. The instructor also described spontaneous effects of his imagery encounters:

> I have received several gifts of great value that result from flashes of intuition. For years I have been germinating a variety of seeds by traditional methods.

> I suddenly come up with a new procedure that eliminates drudgery and risk to plants, and reduces costs. A great burden is lifted from me. Shortly afterward I discover another way to use natural light at no cost, which is superior for plant growth and health. Both of these inventions come through flashes of inspiration.

> These two innovations are equivalent to moving from the horse and buggy to the jet age with my work. Their consequence defies description. I suspect my imagination and creativity are free to work more effectively. I'll wait to see what comes next!

Though his first images were only two blobs, he accepted them with the attitude of an appreciative observer. He worked patiently at home, not stopping after his first imagery exercise in which there was no resolution between the two warring functions. He continued for five days, ten or fifteen minutes a day, and resisted the temptation to discard or analyze them. For a thinking type and a scientist, this was no trivial feat!

After the two were allowed to express their anger toward each other, one feeling overworked (sensing) and the other underused (intuition), hostility resolved into cooperation and inner peace. This often happens when two opposing functions are of unequal strength at the symbolic level so that one is the victim of its dominant counterpart: The weaker one must receive attention and develop before a working relationship can occur. The resolution of this inequality results in a productive and fruitful relationship that, in this case, generated two inventions for the instructor's horticultural work.

The Whispering Bear

Joseph, a 42-year-old intuitive–thinking type, worked as a computer programmer for a Silicon Valley high-tech company. He assessed himself as someone good with ideas, goals, plans, and theories, adding, "I very much enjoy learning about theories and experiments and can mull them over in my head. I think about how I might change them when applying them to my own experiences."

Thinking and Intuition: The Lion and the Dove *(Dominant and Auxiliary Functions)*   Two images appeared that represented Joseph's thinking and intuition: an aggressive lion for thinking, the dominant, and a dove for intuition, the auxiliary. At first, the lion and the dove sat and stared as if they were waiting for him to do something. Suddenly, the lion got up, pushed the imager through the meadow, and complained that he was not being used to the best of his ability. The lion explained that both he and the dove had potent gifts for him if he would trust them and have more self-confidence: "Their gift is that I am powerful and can do a lot of good. I need to trust them more; they will always be beside me. They give me confidence."

Feeling: The Whispering Bear *(Least Preferred Function)*
In the forest, he saw a log cabin surrounded by soft undulat-

ing energy. "Suddenly, the energy rushes from the cabin and enters my chest. It feels wonderful. I am experiencing a revelation about myself, a flash of insight. It is very powerful. I am entering a new realm of consciousness."

In the meadow, the energy took the form of a turtle without a shell and covered with soft hair, seeming vulnerable. The turtle felt "ignored and hurt. It is very willing to give me its gift if I will only listen. It is afraid that I will leave it in the forest to die. Its gift is an understanding of people's feelings, including my own."

On the mountain, the turtle transformed into a teddy bear who wrapped its arms around the imager's neck. It whispered in his ear and told him about his own feelings and those of others. "The teddy bear crawls up onto my shoulders and wraps its paws around my face. It wants to direct my eyes and whisper into my ear about what I should see and how I should feel."

Joseph, who had recently been concerned about personal relationships and his inability to express feelings, offered the following comments and interpretation:

> My girlfriend demands that I tell her what I'm feeling. I usually respond with an idea or by saying nothing. The bear is helping me to understand what I feel and what others feel. It cannot get inside me, but is always on the outside trying to control my head. It is very gentle and understanding. I am trying to listen to it, but I cannot understand a lot of what it is telling me. It caresses my face and head. I feel a lot of love radiating from it.... It is all right to have weaknesses. I now understand my girlfriend better and how she sees me. I hope to keep listening and learning from my bear—I don't plan on leaving my feelings unheard.

Joseph's least preferred function, feeling, appeared first as undulating energy that rushed into his chest, an experience he felt was like entering a new realm of consciousness. It was as though his feeling function arrived, full-blown, to add an expanded power of knowing to his mind.

His new-found function had the quality of adaptability and an empathic understanding of others' feelings. The whispering bear remained "on the outside," telling him what he should feel and what other people were feeling: He learned about feelings by listening and following the directions of the talking bear. Later, as he used the function more, the bear became an integral part of himself rather than one that was outside and separate. Meanwhile, the symbol showed him how to develop this interpersonal skill.

The Images of Feeling Types
ESFJ, ENFJ, ISFP, INFP

Images for the feeling function often have an intimacy or softness that may be associated with certain animals or birds. They also show a quality of openness characterized by, for example, a vase or flowers. Examples include a deer and fawn, a teddy bear, a squirrel, a violet light from a campfire, a small fountain of water, an angel, a white bird, a vase, a red rose, a white horse, a dove, a pond, a stag with velvety antlers, and a turtle.

Breaking the Ball and Chain

The following example shows the kind of personal knowledge that images might bring. Sharon is a 37-year-old police officer, an intuitive–feeling type, who had worked for the past five years as a deputy sheriff on patrol. She described herself as outgoing and decisive. "When I first became a deputy, I submerged myself in my job almost to the exclusion of my husband. I had new friends and a purpose in life. The power and control I had over others was euphoric!"

One day, after witnessing a suicide and murder, she came home and began to cry uncontrollably. The following day, her "rage went out of control in physical brutality on an arrestee, one who had caused a near-fatal accident while fleeing in a stolen vehicle. I was so frightened by my outburst, I knew I needed to change. I was compromising my own personal values." She returned to school, finished an undergraduate degree, and entered graduate school to pursue new opportunities in law enforcement.

Feeling: The Budding Rose *(Dominant Function)*   In the forest, her image for feeling was a partly opened rose with a gouge on its upper petals, wounded and alone. In the meadow, the flower took on a brilliant pink hue, opened fully, and was surrounded by other foliage.

The rose said that it needed her soft side to emerge and that it feared being crushed. Its gift was "fulfillment and acceptance as a feminine woman." On the mountain, the flower turned into an eagle and flew toward a rainbow, keeping one wing in contact with the mountain. She interpreted her image this way:

> My professional life as a police officer closed this part of me, and I am working to free its expression. The flower represents my soft side, which is suffering. Years of being tough and critical has squashed this part, even though others view me as warm and caring.

Thinking: The Ball and Chain *(Least Preferred Function)* The image for her thinking function was a ball and chain that she found attached to a steel pole in the forest. In the meadow, the chain links separated, and the ball became transparent. The ball needed freedom and was afraid of being seen as empty, stupid, or shallow. Its gift was "knowledge, courage, and the capacity to seek higher things." On the mountain, "the ball and chain become multicolored balloons attached to a string floating upward." This is how she interpreted her image:

> The ball is my analytical mind, which feels chained and stifled yet desires to be free. I compare myself to others at school and come up short in the thinking area. I fear being seen as empty, shallow, and unthinking. I am afraid I don't measure up, as if someone will find out my secret stupidity. If I don't talk much, this secret will remain intact.

> The gift of my image is the courage to continue developing this part of me, to seek higher knowledge. I am deeply challenged and find validation for who I am. I can think of no greater lesson.

She also reported certain spontaneous effects of her imagery journey. Her attitude toward studies in graduate school began to change. She was more expressive, spoke up in class, and shared her thoughts in ways she had not dared before.

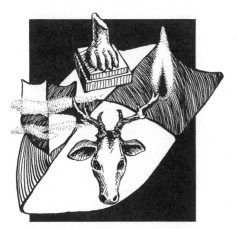

The Shield and Flame

Another way that imagery can help is in relation to distorted type development in which natural strengths are underused and the least preferred functions overused. When this happens, the least preferred functions seem to control. Those whose type development is distorted may have a sense of acting or playing roles in life without truly being themselves. When imagery portrays this, it may help people to redirect life goals and reclaim their type heritage so that chosen activities flow in the direction of psychic energies rather than in opposition to them.

The following example of an intuitive–feeling type illustrates a case in point. Art is a 31-year-old drama critic working for a major metropolitan newspaper. He was raised in a family of sensing–thinking types whose hard-headed realism and objective criticism were taught as the only way to approach life. He adopted this view at an early age to please his family and become successful. Although being a drama critic fit his family's aspirations, he found it a difficult task. "I keep working harder and harder, and my moods get worse and worse. I procrastinate. I feel overrun, confused in my expressions, and have difficulty externalizing my thoughts. My mind goes blank. I am very angry. I am a very critical critic!"

Feeling: A Shield Lost in Fog *(Dominant Function)* In the forest, his image for feeling was a shield hidden in the fog. On the mountain, the fog lifted and a cross appeared on the shield. To him, it meant "the coming together of my faith and deepest feelings. My feelings protect me and give me a weapon to withstand life. Nonetheless, it is so tentative and the shield is so wary of coming out, I wonder what is behind it."

Intuition: A Flame Without a Candle *(Auxiliary Function)* His image for intuition emerged from the forest into the meadow as a flame without a candle. "It is fragile and worried about going out. It asks me to protect it. When we go up the mountain, it turns into a frisky mountain goat urging me to hurry up and join it. My intuition has much more spunk than I thought!"

Though this imager was an intuitive–feeling type, the shield was hidden in fog, and the flame was without structure in the sense that it had no candle to support it. The images of hidden shield and fragile flame graphically reflected the underdevelopment of the two functions and exemplified what Myers (1980) called *distorted type,* which occurs when a person's natural type strengths go undeveloped in childhood.

The fog cleared on the mountain and became a confirmation of the man's feeling type values. The flame without a candle changed into a "spunky" goat, an animal full of energy and agility, easily able to find its way among steep crags. Such symbolic changes suggested what resources were available when natural strengths were developed. This imager went on to seek a new career path that would support his intuition and feeling functions.

Sensing and Thinking: A Tiger's Paw and Silent Elk *(Tertiary and Least Preferred Functions)* Sensing appeared to Art as "a large tiger paw standing in the doorway. It won't move, but there is a tremendous amount of energy flowing through its black and orange colors. To me it means a firm, tiger-gripping steadiness, a rigidity, and an inability to move."

His image of thinking was a large elk. It burst from the door and said nothing. "I am awestruck by his power. In the sunlight I touch him. The elk lets me pet him but will not speak." He reported that this was very much like "my infatuation and awe with ideas. However, when I am able to touch them I understand myself better."

These images reflected the difficulties he faced. His sensing function was the image of a rigid tiger's paw; his thinking function was the image of a silent elk. In experiencing both images, his energy was blocked, frozen, or silent.

On the mountain, he was shown a way to use his thinking function in a manner more compatible to a natural feeling type. He petted the elk and touched it, symbolic of a feeling type's approach to thinking—to experience ideas personally and seek their relevance to individual experience. This contrasted with his present use of thinking, which caused him great stress.

The Ageless Indian Chief

Sometimes when one seeks an image for the dominant function, its opposite will also appear if the relationship between the two hinders the use and expression of the most preferred function. This is illustrated by the case of an intuitive–feeling type, Dan, a 27-year-old teacher and counselor at a community college. He reported that his thinking function caused difficulties when "under a lot of pressure or threatened in some way. I most often strike out at others with a very cold, rational, and cynical analysis of what they are doing or have done."

Feeling and Thinking: A Rabbit Versus Einstein *(Dominant and Least Preferred Functions)*   Dan's image for feeling was a rabbit, and his image for thinking was Einstein. "The rabbit is gray, with large floppy ears and whiskers that drag on the ground. Einstein is an old man who says nothing and looks me over as if to size me up!" Einstein stood behind the rabbit, unable to move unless the rabbit got out of the way. He glanced at the rabbit with an air of disgust and feared that it would be pampered and forced him to remain locked inside a cottage.

In the sunshine, the relationship between Einstein and the rabbit changed. They moved and functioned autonomously, and Einstein became younger and more vibrant.

Then he noticed that his own self-image began to change:

> I see myself as intelligent and cognizant of issues affecting my life. When I am with others, some of the usual conflicts are absent. Up till now, I felt pulled between two ways of being in the world—either with passion or reason. It is as if passion (a sense of being really alive) cannot coexist with reason. This limits

my experience of others and of myself. I am comforted to realize that thinking, for me, can be called
upon in a different way.

Sensing: The Ageless Indian Chief *(Tertiary Function)*
The tertiary function sometimes emerges with considerable
force, particularly at the developmental stage when its use
requires full attention. This imager appeared to be in that
stage, and the following experience with his tertiary function, sensing, illustrates the impact of its symbolic discovery.

In the forest setting, the imager experienced an emerging energy that represented his sensing function:

> There are bubbles coming from between the trees,
> blowing into the meadow where they pop. A strong
> gaseous vapor seeps out from the forest thicket. I
> hear shrill screams and blood-curdling growls. As
> I move closer, I see an apelike creature. It appears
> to be as interested in me as I am in it.

The creature would not come to the meadow, but told
him to be patient and that it would come at another time. Its
gift was

> grounding, enjoyment of the little things, and
> mastery. While climbing the mountain together,
> I notice how ugly and vulgar its mannerisms are.
> It slobbers, grunts, and is incredibly awkward.

> Surprisingly, at the top of the mountain, the creature
> disappeared. In its place stood an ageless Indian
> chief. He was at one with the environment and knew
> the world in a way that afforded him tremendous
> peace and wisdom. Although he said nothing for a
> long time, he was very easy to be with. I was ex
> tremely comforted to find that my higher wisdom,
> my sensing function, was most like the Indian rather
> than the horrid beast of my forest.

Dan offered the following interpretation of the image
for his sensing function:

That the creature turned into an Indian is very significant to me. The Indians' way of being-in-the-world has long symbolized for me the highest state of consciousness when it comes to getting along in the material world. At once, they know intimately the sensing environment and hold the deepest respect and reverence for the objects and events of day-to-day life.

Two weeks following this imagery encounter, he reported that

without understanding how or why, I experience an internal upheaval that is unsettling.... I find myself unable to concentrate on school or relationships. I feel intolerably, pitifully incomplete and have difficulty initiating even the smallest decisions.... I have contacted neglected parts of myself, and they demand attention and expression in my life. My sensing–thinking functions are knocking at the door.

Sometimes when unused functions surface to consciousness, it is temporarily unsettling. For Dan, it lasted for a few short weeks and prompted him to give the unused functions some time and space in his life. That summer he felt a strong need to work with his hands rather than his head, so he went to the mountains and built a cabin, fulfilled by the daily expression of his new sensing function.

This example shows how there can be an outburst of repressed psychic energy when a function emerges at the symbolic level. When this happens, initial disorientation may be followed by complete absorption in the activities associated with the new function.

---■---

Images of the Least Preferred Functions

Several patterns are reflected in the encounters with the tertiary and inferior functions described in the previous examples. Negative attitudes can be changed into more positive ones ("Breaking the Ball and Chain"), the inferior function can help to balance the dominant ("The Questing Knight"), more constructive ways to use the function can be discovered ("Gift of the White Rabbit" and "The Whispering Bear"), distress and tension can result from overuse or underuse of a function ("The Shield and Flame"), and conflicts can be resolved between two auxiliary functions ("The Resolution of Hostile Images").

However, images of the tertiary and inferior functions may also lead to renewal and creativity. Noting the great concentration of life in the least preferred function, von Franz (1971) observed that "as soon as the superior function is worn out—beginning to rattle and lose oil like an old car— if people succeed in turning to their inferior function, they will rediscover a new potential of life" (p. 11).

For some, imaging the third function may be quite similar in experience to that reported by those who image the fourth. This occurs most frequently with imagers in their late twenties when, according to type theory, the third function is ready for further development.

The imagery of the inferior function, and sometimes that of the tertiary, reflects these considerations and so can appear grotesque, hostile, and primitive. As we might expect, these images may arouse some fear or apprehension. Yet they can also enter the area of creative resolution—taken up the mountain or bathed in the sunlight of one's own higher wisdom—and can become benign and helpful, offering unusual gifts for those willing to accept the image with compassion. This is one of the powerful transformative aspects of purposeful imagery—discovering the redeeming qualities of the least preferred functions. Imagery provides a different perspective about the function and a new approach for its use that can encourage its positive development.

In this chapter I have shown how the personal image of a function can enrich our insight and provide a unique understanding of psychological type. We also noted the spontaneous effects that such images generate in both attitudes and behaviors. In the next chapter, our focus is on the deliberate and conscious use of the function's image in appropriate daily life situations.

5

Applications
of the Inner Image

It is equally a grave mistake to think that it is enough to gain some
understanding of the images and that knowledge can here make a half.
Insight into them must be converted into an ethical obligation.
— Jung, 1961, p. 192

THIS CHAPTER WILL examine how the power of the image can be strengthened by using images consciously and deliberately in daily life, not leaving to chance the opportunity to benefit from its influence when using the four functions in everyday living. Evoking a spontaneous image is only the beginning. In order for it to be most meaningful and useful to us, we must consciously use it, nourish it, and apply it in appropriate life situations. In this way, it becomes much more than a solitary insight.

Insights from imagery may initially inspire or rouse us to some form of action. Yet insight is usually brief, like a shooting star that streaks brilliantly through the night sky but soon disappears. Imagery insights may also act in this way, producing a momentary "aha" experience when things suddenly begin to make sense in a new light. Too often, however, the inspiration fades or is dimmed by our habitual responses.

To avoid the fate of short-lived illuminations, the image must be applied to the tasks of daily living—must be at the service of conscious choice and use. When this happens, the imager has the opportunity to shift from an automatic, habitual response pattern to one that is self-directed.

Conscious application of imagery has been somewhat neglected, perhaps because imagery users have sometimes been distracted by the aura of inspiration surrounding the initial image, then lulled into assuming that such an experience has exhausted the possibilities of the event. Thus, many have experienced images that then slipped back into the unconscious, leaving their gifts unclaimed on the threshold of the conscious mind.

The Image and Conscious Choice: Grounding an Image

To use the image consciously may seem at first like a herculean task. Frequently, the concepts involved in psychological type are easily forgotten in the rush and flow of concrete experience. However, the nature of the image underlying these concepts may come to our assistance in an unexpected way by giving us easier access to the use of each function. In imagery, the impersonal word and the very personal meaning converge as a face, a flower, a mountain stream, a panther. Such personal images are full of positive affect, a feeling of grace or respect, and a singular identification for that which comes from within.

In addition, if images have power and contain their own energy, they can draw to them the appropriate feelings and behaviors associated with the particular function. Because of this, what first appeared to be a herculean task—to use the four functions consciously and deliberately—may after all be within our power.

To use the image in this manner, we must rely on the process of *grounding*. Grounding an image refers to its conscious outward expression so that it has a life beyond insight alone. To use the image consciously, we must bring it to mind at the appropriate time and place. When this occurs, the image will energize the function it represents, bringing together whatever resources we have developed for it—our previous experiences and the current level of functioning—and direct them toward the situation at hand. All functions can be used in this way, even those that may never have been fully expressed. Each function can offer resources to help us meet current needs, no matter what the developmental stage.

Since it takes time to evoke an image for a function, we seldom have the chance to repeat the experience in the rush of daily life. It is thus helpful to register the image at a level closer to daily awareness and more accessible for conscious use. To do this, we must maintain a sufficient relationship with the image so that when we need to, we can readily call it to mind for use. Drawing the image, finding an object that resembles it, naming it, or expressing it outwardly in some other way will allow it to reside closer to the conscious mind and accessible to the will.

The initial grounding of an image gives it an outward representation of some kind, a cue—a symbol of the symbol, so to speak. Then it can be brought into full awareness at the appropriate time and place. This works even when the image is not fully understood.

▶ Using an image expands its meaning

As we use the image, it will clarify meanings that were previously vague, abstract, or mysterious. Applying even a small insight from the imagery experience will begin to unlock the wisdom inherent in that image.

For example, an intuitive–thinking teacher obtained an image of a candelabra for her dominant function, intuition. It emerged slowly, "sprouting leaves, the flames becoming more radiant as the sunlight increases." The image felt significant to her, although she did not understand the meaning of the candelabra or why the leaves and flames became radiant. Several days later, she applied the image when confronting a student in her classroom:

I used the candelabra to help me decide whether to honor a student's request to leave class. My first instinct is frequently one of skepticism when approached by students with special requests. Recalling my radiant candelabra, I felt an inner knowing that it was all right for her to leave.

She realized then what the increasing radiance of the leaves and light meant, namely, that she should be "willing to trust my intuitive insight and let it inform and enlighten my judgment."

Even when the image is understood, new insights come when it is applied. Assagioli (1970) noted that "the technique of consciously utilizing symbols by visualizing them achieves a further integration between the conscious and the unconscious elements of the personality, and to a certain extent between the logical mind and the unconscious nonlogical aspects of the person" (p. 180).

▶ **Application requires commitment**

The key element in Assagioli's comment is the idea to *consciously* use symbols. However, using an image in daily life is never as exciting and inspirational as the original experience with it. We can never draw or describe the image to do it justice; we can never use it consciously and expect to reexperience the full impact of its original inspiration.

For example, one man's image of the feeling function was represented by a breathtaking, shimmering white stallion and he recalled what happened the first time he tried to use it to help him relate more positively with his children after an exhausting day at the office. He reported that when he called on the white stallion that time, he felt no special inner charge of energy. The wonder and awe were gone, and there was no unfolding of hidden meanings. The stallion was not so bright and grand when it reappeared for later use.

The true image of the stallion, with all its intensity, luminosity, and new insights, remained inside this individual. When the image is used in daily life, only a small amount of the whole image is expressed outwardly. That portion of the whole merely stands for the total potential of the function involved. Each time the image is applied, the function is strengthened.

As we can see, applying an image takes commitment, desire, and effort. The rewards may be more subtle, but in the long run they are much more satisfying than the original inspiration that launched the process.

▶ Application needs to be appropriate

Application is most effective when the image is used in a setting that is natural for its expression. For example, if one normally tackles work from an intuitive basis and a task arises that requires more thoroughness and detail, cueing the sensing function and bringing its power to bear on the task would be appropriate.

▶ Begin with small tasks

After choosing the right time and setting, one then needs to consciously disengage oneself from the circumstance by mentally withdrawing for a few moments to bring the image into the mind's eye. It is helpful to begin with small tasks, rather than stressful decisions or crisis situations, because too much anxiety prevents thoughtful use of the image. Facing seemingly insurmountable odds or coping with an unexpected crisis are fortunately rare events in life. When they do come, it is far better to be practiced and prepared since the full resources of a function are required at such times.

It is in the small tasks of life that the best chances for applying imagery are found. For most of us, ordinary events are what give the day its quality—it is here that the four functions may find their fullest development. If we use them consciously in our daily lives, they develop in strength so that when extraordinary events overtake us, we are better prepared to respond successfully to these new demands.

Let us now examine some examples of practical problem solving and decision making where the conscious use of imagery for a particular function is involved. These examples show the use of each function in daily life and are taken from reports written by persons of differing types.

They illustrate how their images have enabled them to use even their tertiary and least preferred functions to solve problems and make decisions. Since the process of evoking and interpreting images has already been discussed, the examples illustrate only the actual application. These examples are taken from over 150 case reports describing the application of the image for each function several times in different situations. The examples fall short in capturing the full experiences of those who participated in the research, yet their successes and failures are quite revealing.

-------■-------

Using Images of Sensing

When an image of sensing is applied, whether it be the dominant or least preferred function, most people are surprised to find that the image produces results outside the ordinary repertoire of their experience. This may be due to one special quality of sensing—the renewed sense of energy that brings one into the here and now, redirecting energy from the past and future into the present. This renewal of energy is illustrated in the following examples.

▶ **In a racquetball game**
   (When sensing is the dominant function)

An athletic coach who was a sensing–feeling type was losing against his opponent in a racquetball game. He became discouraged and wanted to give up. He evoked his image of a vibrant rose, his dominant sensing image, as the game continued. "I see the rose in my mind. After a minute I feel a renewed and refreshed attitude toward the game. I play as hard as I can, and am able to make a comeback and win."

▶ **While grocery shopping**
   (When sensing is the auxiliary function)

An intuitive–thinking type, usually bored by grocery shopping, was particularly irritated one day at the thought of having to spend time in the supermarket. She remembered the image of her auxiliary sensing function, a tightly knit gray sweater, and evoked it just to see what would happen. She described her experience this way:

> I slowly begin to enjoy the task more, noticing the odors of foods, imagining their tastes, touching the fruit, becoming aware of colors.... I still have to do the shopping, but I have more fun with it. It strikes me that changing my attitude toward this and similar tasks, from [one of] obligation to adventure, could leave me more energized and more effective!

▶ **Finishing a term paper**
(When sensing is the tertiary function)

An intuitive–feeling type student, in attempting to meet a term paper deadline, began writing in the only quiet room available, a small student lounge, but was soon interrupted by friends who had come to make coffee and socialize. He quickly became distracted and had difficulty continuing to write. After evoking his sensing image, an eagle, he was able to become oblivious of his surroundings and immersed in his work. "I no longer hear anyone or notice what they are doing. This is an amazing experience." Calling upon his symbol for the sensing function enabled him to mobilize his energy and resume his work, which he finished without further distraction.

▶ **Consulting with a client**
(When sensing is the least preferred function)

A consultant for a high-tech company, who was an intuitive–thinking type, was unable to concentrate during a meeting with an important client. After calling on her image of an old heavy water pipe, she began to experience a number of sensations:

> I feel its dampness, hear the echo of its sound,
> become aware of the rhythm of dripping water,

and notice how my own chair is supporting me. I
am suddenly aware of my client and fully present
to him without further effort. We have a productive
session.

▶ **Fixing a car window**
(When sensing is the least preferred function)

An intuitive–feeling type who knew little about automobile
mechanics discovered that the power window on her new
car had jammed. She phoned the car dealer and learned that
repairs would cost five hundred dollars. Deciding to first
call on her sensing image to see if it would inspire a solution she was able to solve the problem with practicality and
resourcefulness:

My image of pulsating purple and gold light
comes easily to mind. I suddenly remember the
car dealer saying something about closing the
window manually. I go to the garage, find a tool
in my husband's workbench, and try pulling the
window up to close it. After several tries I am
successful! What a boost to my feeling of com-
petence to be able to "conquer" that window! My
symbol challenges me to act rather than to wait
for someone else to do it.

The sensing function's association with practicality was in-
strumental in her ability to solve this problem.

———■———

Using Images of Intuition

Intuition is a function that coordinates the perception of relationships—between ideas, events, or people—that are not
usually rendered by the five senses. It thus finds the common
thread of meaning in seemingly unrelated events. Intuitive
images make it possible to use this resource in ways that can

be just as practical as those of the sensing function. The examples that follow illustrate this helpful aspect of the intuitive function.

▶ **Designing a class session**
(When intuition is the dominant function)

A counselor who was an intuitive–feeling type was faced with the prospect of teaching a college class that seemed poorly organized to him. He was bewildered by the jumbled sequence of materials he was given and questioned his ability to teach the class at all. Evoking his image of intuition, a tall pine tree under which he was able to sit quietly and reflect, he discovered that "moments later, I am able to find the problem spot and arrive at an easy, and I think, brilliant solution. I feel great, and am even getting excited about teaching the class at this point." His intuition allowed him to grasp the entire situation at once and make sense of the information and materials that seemed disparate and chaotic to him.

▶ **Simplifying complex materials**
(When intuition is the auxiliary function)

A technical writer, who was an intuitive–thinking type, struggled one morning trying to synthesize highly complex materials for less advanced readers. After hours of exhausting effort, she reported:

> I call up my intuitive image of a butterfly princess and take several minutes of quiet time to be with her. Afterwards, I am able to create a single, flowing example containing the key information in a way that would be palatable. Before, I had been addressing each concept as a separate entity.... I now see the information as an integrated whole, rather than complex unrelated parts.

Her intuition allowed her to penetrate through the mass of material to arrive at a solution that lent order and direction.

▶ **Finding the way when lost**
  (When intuition is the tertiary function)

An intuitive–thinking type lost his way in the dark one night on a college campus. He needed to find a particular building quickly, but couldn't locate any familiar landmarks. He reported how he used his intuitive image to help:

> I evoke my intuitive image of an aluminum canoe paddling down a river as I approach a crucial deciding point. The image brings a flash of inspiration quite different from the normal map of the campus I carry in my head. I turn left, cutting through a dark center of the grounds, and find myself directly in front of the building.

The intuitive hunch helped him in a very practical way to solve his problem.

▶ **Perspective on an overwhelming week**
  (When intuition is the least preferred function)

A sensing–thinking type, whose image of intuition was a snake coiled in a spiral against a background of stars, panicked one night when she realized all the things to be done during the coming week. She evoked her image of intuition, which told her to slow down and enjoy the peace of the moment. Her intuition allowed her to let go of her worries and take a different perspective on accomplishing her tasks:

> I begin to realize that as the sun rises each day so too would all the things I need to get done. I am able to intuitively look past today with an inner peace that will get me through another week.

---■---

Using Images of Thinking

The thinking function, which enables us to understand ideas and bring a measure of rational order to situations, is experienced in a number of different ways, as shown in the examples that follow.

▶ **Participating in an emotional discussion
(When thinking is the dominant function)**

An intuitive–thinking type found herself quite disconnected in an intense group discussion. She was a new member of the group, having joined with hopes of making meaningful contacts. As the discussion became more emotionally intense, she felt increasingly distant and disappointed and wondered how to leave without attracting attention. Then she decided to use her thinking image of a beautiful gold book and held it in conscious awareness.

Within a few minutes, she found herself engaged in the discussion, "grasping the essence of what is being said" and participating with interest. As the discussion continued, she felt more at ease and shared her own thoughts and feelings. Her image helped her see the thread of logic in this emotionally charged discussion.

She again used her image of the gold book when faced with having to write a paper she had no interest in. After fixing the image in her mind, she reported:

> I somehow am inspired and motivated and begin
> to write. My thinking becomes sharp and clear, and
> the writing goes smoothly. The gold book seems to
> increase both my confidence and my compassion
> vis-à-vis the topic.

▶ **Mastering a complex procedure
(When thinking is the auxiliary function)**

An intuitive–thinking type in charge of employee training at a major computer company enrolled in a training course to learn a difficult new procedure, but found her customary intuitive learning style unsuccessful; she felt she was missing the point completely. In her dismay, she called upon her image for thinking and reported:

> During the second day, I call upon my faun image
> of thinking. As the day goes on, I am able to

successfully understand and apply the concept
the trainer is teaching me. I am delighted that I now
understand how thinking and intuition interrelate.
I can use the faun as a fallback when my intuition
does not serve well.

In this way, intuition and thinking can complement each
other when in the dominant and auxiliary positions, respectively.

▶ **Calming an anxious daughter**
  (When thinking is the tertiary function)

A sensing–feeling type received a phone call from his anxious daughter who had found herself in an unfortunate
dilemma. Having used his image of the thinking function to
respond to her, he reported:

> Instead of being anxious myself, which is typical
> of me in such instances, I call on my thinking
> peacock image. Soon I am calm, and give her
> some logical possibilities to solve the problem.
> I do not attempt to solve the problem for her like
> I usually do. My calm strength and logic seem to
> diffuse her anxiety. I feel so relieved and experience
> a positive connection with her.

His thinking function enabled him to distance himself
from the situation enough that he could offer her sound
advice on her problem without actually solving it for her.

▶ **Resolving employee conflicts**
  (When thinking is the least preferred function)

A sensing–feeling type who managed a large health club was
having difficulty with some of his employees. He knew the
existing system of resolving staff conflicts was not working
and needed to make a clear proposal for necessary changes,
but this seemed especially difficult:

> I write down my ideas of possible solutions and
> consequences. Then I walk away and ask my
> thinking bow and arrow image to help organize

my ideas. Soon I am able to see the center focus from which I can outline a new proposal that delineates all the facts.

On another occasion, he evoked the same image to confront an emotionally volatile employee who had accused him of being prejudiced about his background. Though his own emotions rose in response, he took the time to use his image, then found himself "in a gentle confrontation." He was then able to explain how the employee may have misinterpreted his comments:

It proves to be surprisingly helpful. He calms down and we actually have a good evaluation session about his job possibilities. The image helps me use my thinking when I would have normally exploded or dismissed the employee without dealing with the problem.

These illustrations show how the thinking function is particularly adept at objective analysis of complex situations. When it is the least preferred function, its gifts are surprising, even at an elementary level.

---■---

Using Images of Feeling

A significant aspect of the feeling function is its concern with personal values and how such values can have an influence in important relationships. Feeling values tend to facilitate empathic understanding of others and a more sensitive approach to human situations.

▶ **Changing a macho man
(When feeling is the dominant function)**

An intuitive–feeling type, a self-described "macho man," began to question his own behavior toward women after having met a woman he hoped to have a serious relationship with. He decided to seek help from his two feeling images— a white, vibrant ball of light and a gentle doe:

In this new relationship, my doe [image] helps
me show the depth of my feelings in a much softer
and more genuine way. I can allow myself to be
vulnerable and expose my true qualities instead of
my macho personality. A new sense overcomes me
that I like very much.

▶ **Meeting with a school principal**
(When feeling is the auxiliary function)

An intuitive–feeling type teacher met with her school principal with whom she previously had had a number of conflicts.
This time she wanted to make clear suggestions and to work
more harmoniously with her. She evoked her image of
feeling, a humorous snake, and it helped her to respond more
successfully:

I visualize my humorous snake for several
minutes beforehand. Two unusual things begin
to happen during the meeting—my principal
gives me numerous compliments and I feel clear-
headed and assertive about what I want. We have
the most productive meeting ever. It feels like a
real triumph!

▶ **A conflict between values and friendship**
(When feeling is the tertiary function)

A sensing–thinking type used his feeling image of a spiral
of energy surrounding his body to make a difficult decision. This decision involved a conflict of values between
helping a close friend and maintaining his own sense of
integrity:

I go back and forth, weighing the advantages and
disadvantages, but am really caught. Finally I stop,
close my eyes, and bring my spiral image into focus.
I am able to sort my feelings and decide the most
appropriate action to take. I decide not to go against
my values even though I want to help my friend.

This image was successful in helping him clarify his personal
values.

▶ **Handling an angry phone call**
(When feeling is the least preferred function)

An intuitive–thinking type responded antagonistically to a friend who had become angry and critical over the telephone. When he felt his anger rise, he stopped, evoked his image of feeling, which was a blue water-filled vase, and began to let go of his negative feelings:

> I rather quickly become more accepting towards him. It doesn't seem to matter that he is being critical right now. I can choose to feel warmly toward him in spite of it. This saves me from being emotionally embroiled and getting into a fight.

▶ **Listening differently to a critical speaker**
(When feeling is the least preferred function)

A sensing–thinking businesswoman attended a business meeting where a rather critical and stubborn speaker spoke for what seemed a long time. The businesswoman began to suspect that more was going on than simply the speech, and she wished she could understand the speaker's feelings. She used her feeling image of a deer to help her listen differently. "I begin to hear a quiver in the speaker's voice that I'd not perceived; hearing unspoken emotion, I find myself responding empathically."

———■———

Limitations in the Use of Imagery

Any approach that involves the inner image and its use in the outer world will have limitations in its effectiveness from time to time. Imagers vary in their abilities not only to evoke, relate to, and interpret their own internal symbols, but also in their motivation to use such symbols consciously. Other factors in the use of imagery also require special consideration. I have selected a number of these concerns for discussion.

General Problems Related to Type

Difficulties in using sensing images are most likely to arise when sensing is the tertiary or inferior function. Some people are simply unable to evoke a sensing symbol, or one sufficiently strong to be applied, especially when they are in their late twenties. This is when sensing, as the third function, has been relatively unused.

Difficulties associated with the thinking function are also most likely when thinking is the tertiary or inferior function. These difficulties usually involve neglect, suppression, or devaluation of the thinking process.

In contrast, stumbling blocks with intuition are generally found when intuition is dominant or auxiliary and thus more fully developed. These blocks concern such issues as mistrust of intuitive knowledge, fear of perceiving something unfavorable or negative, or uncertainty about whether an insight is intuitive or purely "psychic."

Problems in the use of the feeling function are also most likely found when feeling is the dominant or auxiliary function. In these cases, feeling types may find it difficult to decide whether the image is really having an effect or if they are simply acting out of habit.

Particular Problems Not Related to Type

Other problems can come up that don't specifically relate to a type or function. Rather, they may involve (a) applying an image before it is fully assimilated into consciousness, (b) an inability to sustain an image in conscious awareness, (c) difficulty in obtaining a sufficiently energized image, (d) conflict or intrusion of one image on another, when there are two for the same function, and (e) failure of an image to reflect the quality needed for a particular use.

▶ Applying an image before it is assimilated

The amount of time required to assimilate an image varies greatly and depends on both the individual and the particular image. For many people, assimilation can happen within a few hours; others may require days, weeks, or even months. This is particularly true when the image is charged with strong positive or negative affect: The stronger the affect, the longer the time needed to assimilate the image.

For example, several days after her imagery experience, an intuitive–thinking type was unable to evoke and apply her image of two glowing eyes outlined in a somber face.

> I have not been able to recreate the image. I have such strong positive feelings toward it that I need to further explore this inner connection. The experience is too much to assimilate all at once.

This individual correctly decided that she needed more time to secure her image in conscious thought before attempting to use it.

▶ **Difficulty in sustaining an image**

If the imagery experience does not include some meaningful relationship between the imager and the image, the image may not make a strong enough impression for its presence to be fixed in the mind and retrieved for later use. One should not expect to sustain all four images of the four functions; one is fortunate to have two or three images energized strongly enough to empower their respective functions.

An intuitive–thinking type described the difficulty in sustaining an image in the following way:

> In some situations I cannot sustain the imagery long enough to relate to it; at other times, I am confused as to whether I should retrieve the actual image or its message. There is a difference depending on which of these I focus on. I find that when I recall an image plus its meaning, that this is more effective.

▶ **Difficulty in obtaining
an image strong enough to use**

Sometimes it is difficult to obtain an image that is strong enough to be used later on. This happens when a function has been neglected, and there are minimal inner experiential resources to be harnessed. If an image for a function is not highly energized, it is best used in tranquil situations where the dominant function can rest while its weaker opposite can be coaxed into play.

For example, a sensing–feeling type tried to use a more intuitive approach in an encounter with her son. Intuition was her least preferred, least developed function, and the situation was charged with much concern and anxiety. Her image, however, was unable to help in this case.

> My intuition is not yet powerful enough to
> override my dominant sensing reactions. I try to
> use it when talking with my son, but cannot change
> my usual lecturing behavior. I do feel for the first
> time, however, that I can develop my intuition if
> I give it some attention.

▶ **When two images of the same function
conflict or intrude**

The image for a function obtained in the forest or basement setting, as we have seen, is related to the past and thus may carry unresolved conflicts about how we responded to that function in childhood. In some cases, negative feelings are sufficiently strong to intrude from time to time. The imager still remembers the painful childhood experiences with that function, and such memories result in a conflict between the image obtained in the forest and the current image for the function.

For example, two symbols for an intuitive–thinking type's thinking function, a tiger and a cub, flashed back and forth in her mind's eye when she tried to use that function. The tiger, who reminded her of her father in early childhood, interfered with the cub, her current image of thinking:

> In the forest, the tiger stands strong as if he were
> going to attack me. On the mountain, the area of
> creative resolution, he transforms into a cub and
> cuddles up to me to gain strength. I seem to shift

back and forth between the confusion of the forest experience and the confidence of the mountain. As a child, many of my spoken thoughts and opinions were so criticized by my father, I continually question my own judgment.

▶   **Need for a more appropriate symbol**

A symbol obtained for a function may not be the most useful one with which to develop that function. This judgment is not a matter of preference for one symbol or another but rather one of the image's effectiveness in reflecting those qualities of the function needed in daily life.

This is clearly illustrated by the experience of a sensing–feeling type who used her image of the feeling function to resolve a conflict about buying a house:

> I try using my symbol of a restless bird, my image for feeling, in a conflict with my husband about what kind of house to buy. I begin by calmly stating my needs, but then fly off the handle at my husband for his resistance. I need to find a better symbol for my feeling function that will ground and calm me. My restless bird accurately describes how I use my feeling function, but it is too unpredictable to sustain when I need to call on it.

Other problems reported by imagers have included difficulty in recalling the image in a stressful moment, inability to recall the image at all, paying more attention to the symbol than to the task at hand, and uncertainty as to whether the image actually had an effect.

Positive Effects of Using Imagery

Although certain limitations and problems exist in the use of imagery with psychological type, they are surpassed by the positive effects. The excerpts below are taken from the reports of persons who had such experiences. Effects range from a feeling of calm and peace when evoking an image to surprise at the practicality of using imagery with a function. In several examples, the imager goes beyond practicality to an appreciation of the potential that lies in the inner world. These effects were considered unexpected gifts by the imagers, and I have cited them as I received them, without explanation or further description.

▶ **The gift of peace**
(From a sensing–feeling type)

Every time I recall the image I feel relaxed and comfortable with myself. I feel more peaceful and tend to believe things will work out all right. There is a sense of relief, as if a great burden has been lifted off my shoulders.

▶ **The gift of practicality**
(From an intuitive–feeling type)

Perhaps the most valuable thing for me was the tangibility of labeling a given image for future use. When I did call on that image, it was instantly available. I could see the whole thing all over again. It is such a paradox that something so abstract can be so concrete!

▶ **The invitation to explore**
(From a sensing–thinking type)

Being the skeptic that I am, I find this imagery amazing. When I think of the image I feel this enormous amount of energy. It is frightening! I can feel the force of the waters in every part of my body. It is as though I become one with the image. I still hold back sometimes. I wonder where the waters could take me if I gave in totally and completely.

▶ **A glimpse of integration**
(From an intuitive–feeling type)

My strongest response is that the four images in
my mind seem to have awakened my ability to use
all four functions more effectively and at will than
before. I feel more integrated in terms of an
awareness and use of all parts of me.

▶ **The gift of self-discipline**
(From an intuitive–feeling type)

My four symbols, now that I have assimilated
them, are acting like talismans or totems to guide
and protect me as I approach the variety of tasks
each day. The exercise has taught me how to isolate
each function and get to know its individual
strengths and weaknesses. I feel more disciplined
and effective in reaching into my inner resources
to handle myself well.

▶ **A glimpse of higher connections**
(From an intuitive–thinking type)

This experience was all new to me, yet I had a
feeling of strange familiarity with it. I have thought
about myself during these exercises as I have never
done before. Feelings, ideas, and insights that had
lurked vaguely within me before were made clear
and real. I realize that connections are being made
not just on an ordinary level, but on a higher level
of consciousness, in which possibility and reality
expand.

▶ **The gift of getting started**
(From an intuitive–feeling type)

I'm thrilled to be doing this work. I've had a vague
feeling that there is a gift available to me in symbols
but didn't know how or where to start. Thank you
so much for this opportunity.

---■---

Summary and Speculations

We have just examined the deliberate application of using the inner image with the four cognitive functions of the mind in daily life. It is interesting to note that imagers were able to do this with all four functions, including the least preferred. Such efforts complete the image cycle that begins by going within, evoking a spontaneous image for a cognitive function, interpreting its meaning within the context of type theory, and then applying the image to an external and appropriate task. In this way, both the inner image and the cognitive function are strengthened and developed. This exercise bridges the inner and the outer and helps them work together as partners for growth.

This independent and deliberate use of the image with its respective cognitive function is similar to the specialized mental training of athletes, musicians, and others concerned with increasing the quality of their performance. Such use allows the mind to take a stride forward in reaching its own potential. It also empowers people to use psychological type to go beyond just describing personality characteristics and differences to actively developing full type potential.

The research thus far is based primarily on the self-reports of the imagers. The subjective nature of the inner image lends itself to this means of assessment. Because the symbol system can only be partially understood by the rational mind, there will always be unanswered questions and an aura of some mystery in precisely detailing the effects of a spontaneous image. If experience shows that in most cases the image assists you to more fully develop the gifts of your mind, then there is considerable merit in using imagery even if its inner process is not fully understood.

Finally, for those who have experienced the full impact of the inner image, either in terms of psychological type, personal therapy, or some other context, we would be devaluing their experience if we stopped at the point of saying that the image helped in the attainment of some outer goal, such as type development or the resolution of a problem. That is certainly part of the experience. The other part of the imagery experience goes quite beyond this and reminds us that the inner world does not exist simply to serve the outer. It has a life of its own, and though it may be called upon from time to time to serve goals in the outer world, such service is secondary to its major contribution.

If the image of a cognitive function helps us to use and strengthen that function, then it has graciously introduced itself to us by doing so. Its major contribution is in calling our attention to the world within, beckoning us to listen and understand this hidden part of the self. For the image is the natural language system of the inner world, whose power and meaning are often ignored. Experience testifies that the inner image is really a troubadour that gives poetic expression to a far more profound and mysterious journey than any we might make in the outer world. It sings the songs and echoes the silence that brings us to a fuller knowledge of the self, and as such, acts as a guide to those who seek healing, wholeness, and their pathway home.

References

Achterberg, J. (1985). *Imagery in healing.* Boston: New Science Library.

Assagioli, R. (1970). *Psychosynthesis: A manual of principles and techniques.* New York: Viking.

Crampton, M. (1969, Fall). The use of mental imagery in psychosynthesis. *Journal of Humanistic Psychology.*

Crampton, M. (1978). *An historical survey of mental imagery techniques in psychotherapy and description of the dialogic imagery method.* Paper published by the Quebec Institute of Psychosynthesis, Montreal, Quebec.

Desoille, R. (1968). *The directed daydream.* New York: Psychosynthesis Research Foundation.

Forisha, B. (1979). The outside and the inside: Compartmentalization or integration? In A. Sheikh & J. Shaffer (Eds.), *The potential of fantasy and imagination.* New York: Brandon House.

Fretigny, R., & Virel, A. (1968). *L'imagerie mentale.* Geneva: Mont-Blanc.

Jacobson, E. (1942, 1983). *Progressive relaxation.* Chicago: University of Chicago Press.

Johnson, R. (1986). *Inner work: Using dreams and active imagination for personal growth.* New York: Harper & Row.

Jung, C. G. (1960). The structure and dynamics of the psyche (Tr. by R. F. C. Hull). *Collected works, Vol. 8.* Princeton, NJ: Princeton University Press.

Jung, C. G. (1961). *Memories, dreams, reflections* (Ed. by A. Jaffe). New York: Random House.

Jung, C. G. (1971). *Psychological types*. London: Routledge & Kegan.

Keirsey, D., & Bates, M. (1984). *Please understand me*. Del Mar, CA: Prometheus Nemesis.

Leuner, H. (1969). Guided affective imagery (GAI): A method of intensive psychotherapy. *American Journal of Psychotherapy, 23* (1), 4–22.

Mamchur, C. M. (1984). *Insights: Understanding yourself and others*. Ontario: The Ontario Institute for Studies and Education.

Myers, I. (1980). *Gifts differing*. Palo Alto, CA: Consulting Psychologists Press.

Newman, J. (1985, Fall). The four functions as cognitive processes. *Bulletin of Psychological Type, 7* (1),10–12.

Newman, J. (1986a, Spring). Sensation as a cognitive process. *Bulletin of Psychological Type, 8* (2), 10–12.

Newman, J. (1986b, Fall). Intuition as a cognitive process. *Bulletin of Psychological Type, 9* (1), 4–6.

Newman, J. (1987a, Summer). Thinking as a cognitive process. *Bulletin of Psychological Type, 10* (2), 13, 25–27.

Newman, J. (1987b, Winter). Feeling as a cognitive process. *Bulletin of Psychological Type, 10* (1), 17–20.

Penfield, W., & Perot, P. (1963). The brain's record of auditory and visual experience. *Brain, 86*, 595–596.

Pribram, K. (1971). *Languages of the brain*. Monterey, CA: Brooks/Cole.

Rossman, M. (1984). Imagine health! Imagery in medical self-care. In A. Sheikh (Ed.), *Imagination and healing*. New York: Baywood Publishing.

Samuels, M., & Samuels, N. (1975). *Seeing with the mind's eye*. New York: Random House.

Sheikh, A., & Jordan, C. (1983). Clinical uses of mental imagery. In A. Sheikh (Ed.), *Imagery: Current theory, research, and application*. New York: Wiley.

Sperry, R. W., & Gazzaniag, M. S. (1967). Language following surgical disconnection of the hemispheres. In F. L. Darley (Ed.), *Brain mechanisms underlying speech and language* (pp. 108–121). New York: Grune & Stratton.

Van der Hoop, J. (1939). *Conscious orientation.* New York: Harcourt Brace Jovanovich.

Vaughan, F. (1979). *Awakening intuition.* New York: Anchor Books.

Von Franz, M., & Hillman, J. (1971). *Jung's typology.* New York: Spring Publications.

Watkins, M. (1984). *Waking dreams* (3rd ed.). New York: Spring Publications.

Watkins, M. (1986). *Invisible guests.* Hillsdale, NJ: Erlbaum.

Whitmont, E. (1969). *The symbolic quest.* Princeton, NJ: Princeton University Press.

Appendix

———■———

Selected Resources for an
Understanding of Psychological Type

Grant, H., Thompson, M., & Clarke, T. **From Image to Likeness.** New York: Paulist Press, 1983. The spiritual dimension of Jung's typology is sensitively portrayed within a biblical context. The appendix includes the theory and stages of development for each of the sixteen types throughout the life span.

Hirsh, S., & Kummerow, J. **Lifetypes.** New York: Warner Books, 1989. A discussion of the sixteen types as they interact in the work setting, in leisure activities, and in loving, learning, and communicating. Presents a down-to-earth portrait of psychological type in action with cases, illustrations, and practical suggestions for its constructive use.

Jung, C. G. **Psychological Types.** London: Routledge & Kegan, 1971. Jung's original work on type and function written in 1921. His type descriptions are still classic and surprisingly accurate. Historical and philosophical sources along with some case histories are included.

Lawrence, G. **People Types & Tiger Stripes.** Gainesville, FL: CAPT, 1979. Application of Jungian typology to education, teaching, and parenting. Included are self-analysis questions, a basic type concepts quiz, classroom applications, and ways to plan instruction so that all types benefit.

Myers, I. **Gifts Differing.** Palo Alto, CA: Consulting Psychologists Press, 1980. Summary of insights gained from research based on the *Myers-Briggs Type Indicator* and personal experience. Written in a clear and concise style, this is an excellent overview to the understanding of Jung's typology as modified and expanded by Isabel Myers.

Myers, I. **Introduction to Type.** Palo Alto, CA: Consulting Psychologists Press, 1980. An introductory pamphlet giving brief descriptions of types, the type table, and a number of suggested applications.

Von Franz, M., & Hillman, J. **Jung's Typology.** New York: Spring Publications, 1971. An in-depth discussion of the inferior and feeling functions by two highly respected Jungian writers.

Yaker, H., Desmond, H., & Cheek, F. (Eds.). **The Future of Time**. New York: Anchor Press, 1972. The chapter on the psychotypology of time is a fascinating report on the four major frames of reference: sensing, intuition, thinking, and feeling. The authors describe the unique concept of time and space for each dominant viewpoint. Includes a number of practical insights and applications.

———■———

Selected Resources for an Understanding of Spontaneous Imagery

Achterberg, J. **Imagery in Healing.** Boston: New Science Library, 1985. An informative summary of the history and current research into the healing power of the image, its physiological and biochemical base, and its uses in medicine, psychotherapy, and other forms of the healing arts.

Assagioli, R. **Psychosynthesis.** New York: Viking Press, 1970. A systematic approach to the integration of the personal and transpersonal domains in psychology. Of particular relevance are the sections on symbol utilization and initiated symbol projection.

Johnson, R. **Inner Work: Using Dreams and Active Imagination for Personal Growth.** New York: Harper & Row, 1986. The author gives practical steps in understanding and interpreting dreams and images through the eyes of Jung's active imagination process. Chapter 3 is particularly helpful in interpreting imagery in a four-step approach.

Samuels, M., & Samuels, N. **Seeing with the Mind's Eye.** New York: Random House, 1975. Surveys the use of imagery in medicine, psychology, science, religion, and the arts. Of particular interest are chapters 13 and 14 showing the use of imagery in psychology and medicine. Heavily illustrated with photographs and drawings.

Sheikh, A., & Shaffer, J. (Eds.). **The Potential of Fantasy and Imagination.** New York: Brandon House, 1979. A review of various approaches in the imagery field. Chapter 1 by Forisha is particularly helpful in understanding the relationship between the semantic and symbolic language systems.

Watkins, M. **Waking Dreams.** New York: Spring Publications, Third Edition, 1984. Reviews the history of imagery and explores the dimensions, interpretations, and approaches to guided spontaneous imagery, contrasting the American and European approaches. Highly recommended.

Watkins, M. **Invisible Guests: The Development of Imaginal Dialogues.** Hillsdale, NJ: The Analytic Press, 1986. A penetrating analysis of various psychological theories and the imagery system, ending with a reconception of developmental theory and imaginal dialogues with the inner image.

About the Author

WILLIAM YABROFF RECIEVED his doctorate in counseling psychology from Stanford University. He is on the graduate faculty of Santa Clara University and the Fielding Institute. He has served on the National Council of the Association of Psychological Type as Theory Interest Coordinator, and is a faculty member of the Center for Applications of Psychological Type (CAPT).

He has extensive experience training clinicians and others in the therapeutic uses of imagery and symbol throughout the country, as well as using psychological type in consulting and teaching. His current pioneering work in the imagery field is based on a six-year research project at Santa Clara University, exploring the uses of personal inner symbols in the development of psychological type.

William, an INFP, enjoys creating music on the synthesizer, boating in the San Francisco Bay, and making pilgrimages to lands where ancient symbols retain their power, such as in Egypt, India, and Italy. One of his most recent journeys was to Egypt, where he co-led a study tour for the New York Jung Foundation and the Fielding Institute.